"The way of Advent is the way of waiting. In this guide through Advent's ancient prayers and practices, Tish Harrison Warren teaches us why we wait and how we wait for the One who was and is and is to come. Come, Lord Jesus!"

Joel Scandrett, associate professor of historical theology at Trinity School for Ministry

"In *Advent*, Tish Harrison Warren writes with her signature warmth, insight, and intelligence. Her effort to 'make Christmas weird again' succeeds from start to finish. Everything Tish writes is a must-read, and this book is no exception."

Andrea Palpant Dilley, online managing editor of *Christianity Today*

"Much like Mozart's music and Shakespeare's plays, the season of Advent satisfies at so many different levels—theologically, imaginatively, affectively, ethically, liturgically, and so on. In this beautifully compact book, Tish Harrison Warren invites readers to experience the multilevel richness of Advent and to discover thereby the full richness of the triune God. *Tolle lege*, friends; take up and read, and let Christ himself fill you to the fullest with a life that was and is and is yet to come."

W. David O. Taylor, associate professor of theology and culture at Fuller Theological Seminary and author of *Open and Unafraid*

"Like myself, many Christians in the United States today did not grow up in traditions that practiced the liturgical calendar. For us, Tish Harrison Warren's book *Advent* is a godsend because it makes the spirituality and practices of the season relevant and accessible. Finally, a book relating to Christian spiritual formation that is rooted in the great tradition of the church!"

Kurtley Knight, assistant professor of spiritual formation at George Fox University's Portland Seminary

"What a rich work that encourages deep discipleship, as Tish Harrison Warren invites us to remember that learning to wait with hope is central to following Jesus Christ. In this world where darkness often seems stronger than light, Warren reminds us that throughout the centuries Advent has been a time to look honestly at the darkness while attending to the light of Christ, our true hope. In this cultural moment marked by impatience, this book encourages us to receive Advent as a training in patience and hope. Christians who have long practiced Advent and those who might be considering it for the first time will find in this volume a beautiful and timely invitation to embrace it as a means of grace."

Kristen Deede Johnson, G. W. and Edna Haworth Professor of Educational Ministries and Leadership at Western Theological Seminary and author of *The Justice Calling*

Esau McCaulley, SERIES EDITOR

Tish Harrison Warren

WITH CONTRIBUTIONS BY Jonathan Warren Pagán

Advent

The Season of Hope

Fullness of Time series

An imprint of InterVarsity Press
Downers Grove, Illinois

InterVarsity Press
P.O. Box 1400 | Downers Grove, IL 60515-1426
ivpress.com | email@ivpress.com

InterVarsity Press® is the publishing division of InterVarsity Christian Fellowship/USA®. For more information, visit intervarsity.org.

All Scripture quotations, unless otherwise indicated, are taken from The Holy Bible, New International Version®, NIV®. Copyright © 1973, 1978, 1984, 2011 by Biblica, Inc.™ Used by permission of Zondervan. All rights reserved worldwide. www.zondervan.com. The "NIV" and "New International Version" are trademarks registered in the United States Patent and Trademark Office by Biblica, Inc.™

While any stories in this book are true, some names and identifying information may have been changed to protect the privacy of individuals.

The publisher cannot verify the accuracy or functionality of website URLs used in this book beyond the date of publication.

Cover design: David Fassett
Interior design: Daniel van Loon

ISBN 978-1-5140-0-0018-2 (print) | ISBN 978-1-5140-0-0019-9 (digital)

Printed in the United States of America ∞

Library of Congress Cataloging-in-Publication Data
Names: Harrison Warren, Tish, 1979- author.
Title: Advent : the season of hope / Tish Harrison Warren ; with
    contributions Jonathan Warren Pagan.
Description: Downers Grove, IL : InterVarsity Press, [2023] | Series: The
    fullness of time | Includes bibliographical references.
Identifiers: LCCN 2023006659 (print) | LCCN 2023006660 (ebook) | ISBN
    9781514000182 (print) | ISBN 9781514000199 (digital)
Subjects: LCSH: Advent.
Classification: LCC BV40 .H358 2023 (print) | LCC BV40 (ebook) | DDC
    242/.332—dc23/eng/20230417
LC record available at https://lccn.loc.gov/2023006659
LC ebook record available at https://lccn.loc.gov/2023006660

29   28   27   26   25   24   23 | 11   10   9   8   7   6   5   4   3   2   1

To Woody Giles, who has taught us
about waiting with hope and joy.
Beloved friend, let's wait together.

"En estos dias,
a los abatidos nos toca fijar los ojos
en una gloria palpable, intolerable:
algo capaz de rescatarnos de duras posibilidades
e introducir nuestras almas a la realidad
de una celebración que nunca muere
y un amor no pasajero."

But we have a promise upon which to base our hope:

The promise of his love.

So our life can rightly be a waiting in expectation, but waiting patiently and with a smile. Then, indeed, we shall be really surprised and full of joy and gratitude when he comes.

HENRI NOUWEN, *THE GENESEE DIARY*

Contents

The Fullness of Time

SERIES PREFACE

ESAU MCCAULLEY, SERIES EDITOR

Christians of all traditions are finding a renewed appreciation for the church year. This is evident in the increased number of churches that mark the seasons in their preaching and teaching. It's evident in the families and small groups looking for ways to recover ancient practices of the Christian faith. This is all very good. To assist in this renewal, we thought Christians might find it beneficial to have an accessible guide to the church year, one that's more than a devotional but less than an academic tome.

The Fullness of Time project aims to do just that. We have put together a series of short books on the seasons and key events of the church year, including Advent,

Christmas, Epiphany, Lent, Easter, and Pentecost. These books are reflections on the moods, themes, rituals, prayers, and Scriptures that mark each season.

These are not, strictly speaking, devotionals. They are theological and spiritual reflections that seek to provide spiritual formation by helping the reader live fully into the practices of each season. We want readers to understand how the church is forming them in the likeness of Christ through the church calendar.

These books are written from the perspective of those who have lived through the seasons many times, and we'll use personal stories and experiences to explain different aspects of the season that are meaningful to us. In what follows, do not look for comments from historians pointing out minutiae. Instead, look for fellow believers and evangelists using the tool of the church year to preach the gospel and point Christians toward discipleship and spiritual formation. We pray that these books will be useful to individuals, families, and churches seeking a deeper walk with Jesus.

Yearning

THREE ADVENTS OF CHRIST

As the calendar year winds down, as the days darken and grow short, as Christmas songs spill from crowded stores and children set about making wish lists for Santa, the church's year dawns. On the fourth Sunday before Christmas, Advent begins. The first day of Advent is our Christian New Year's Day. It kicks off the entire cycle of the liturgical calendar, which through each passing week will slowly unfurl the story of Jesus' life, death, resurrection, ascension, and sending of the Holy Spirit.

We begin our Christian year in waiting. We do not begin with our own frenetic effort or energy. We do not begin with the merriment of Christmas or the triumph of Easter. We do not begin with the work of the church or the mandate of the Great Commission. Instead, we begin in a place of yearning. We wait for our king to come.

The word *advent* derives from the Latin *adventus*, which means "coming." The liturgical season of Advent is the time in which we prepare for and look forward to the coming of Christ.

Christians, of course, believe that Christ has already come. Jesus has already brought the kingdom of God near. He has already stretched out his hands to heal and to bless. He has already been broken on the cross and defeated death. He has already poured out his Spirit. So why do we reenter a season of waiting each year? What are we waiting for?

We Christians believe, however, not just in one coming of Christ but in three: the coming of Christ in the incarnation (theologians have sometimes called this the *adventus redemptionis*, the coming of redemption), the coming of Christ in what Scripture terms "the last days" (the *adventus glorificamus*, the coming in glory), and the coming of Christ in our present moment, through the Holy Spirit's work and through Word and sacrament (the *adventus sanctificationis,* the coming of holy things or holiness).[1] Advent celebrates and holds together all three "comings" of Christ.

It is a deeply paradoxical season, at once past, present, and future. Ancient yet urgent.

When we enter into the waiting of Advent, we do so not primarily as individuals but with all people of faith throughout time and around the globe. When we worship together each week, we join our voices, as the Anglican liturgy says, "with angels and archangels and the whole company of heaven."[2] Because of this, the church calendar as a whole—and Advent specifically—is a way to reach toward timelessness through time itself. It is a season marked by days and weeks, yet through it we enter into the eternal story of God and God's work on earth.

The Coming of Christ in the Incarnation

In Advent we intentionally join our brothers and sisters in the Old Testament who waited faithfully for the Messiah to come. We seek to enter their perspective and take on their posture. Of course, we live our lives in AD, in the year of our Lord, not BC. But "Advent itself is always BC!" writes Malcolm Guite. "The whole purpose of Advent is to be for a moment fully and consciously Before Christ."[3]

We know that Christ has come, and yet the season of Advent calls us out of our time-bound moment to remember and perform the whole drama of Scripture. Through the liturgical calendar we don't merely retell the story of the gospel; we enter it. In this way the church calendar is like immersive theater.[4]

In immersive theater, no one is simply a spectator watching a play. The distinction between actors and audience is broken down and everyone becomes a character in the story. In the same way, in Advent we join the people of Israel waiting for the coming Messiah. We reenact their yearning for and anticipation of the coming king. Though we now know the story of Christmas—the story of Jesus' first coming—we imaginatively enter into the confusion, longing, frustration, and sense of dreams deferred that the people of Israel felt year after year, generation after generation. We prepare for the joy of Christmas by waiting on the dark streets of Bethlehem, our eyes straining to glimpse the dawning of that everlasting light.

In the book of Luke, Jesus has a strange exchange with the Sadducees where he points out that Moses called the Lord "the God of Abraham, and the God of Isaac, and the God of Jacob." Then Jesus says, "He is not the God of the dead, but of the living, for to him all are alive" (Luke 20:37-38). Because "to him all are alive," the God we worship is still the God of Abraham, still the God of Isaac, still the God of Jacob. So even though we live two thousand years after Jesus' birth, it is appropriate—even vital—for us to join in the ache of these Old Testament saints, not only in our imaginations but through the mysterious reality of the communion of saints across time. When we participate in the season of Advent we are taking part in the corporate longing of Abraham, Isaac, Jacob, Rahab, Moses, Miriam, Isaiah, and Ruth. We are bearing their burdens and their stories.

In the medieval church, as the season of Advent was taking shape, Christians developed a pattern of praying together seven prayers that reference descriptions of the Messiah from the Old Testament. These prayers are poetry, telling us what Christ is like through metaphor without saying the name of Jesus directly. Instead they call to Jesus using other names given in Scripture: "O Wisdom!" "O Adonai!" "O Root!" "O Key!" "O Light!" "O King of the Nations!" "O Emmanuel!"

These are called the "O Antiphons" because the church sang these prayers antiphonally, back and forth, by call and response. They are now sung by some churches on the seven days leading up to Christmas Eve. Many churches, however, have lost this ancient practice, but an echo of the tradition remains in the beloved Advent hymn "O Come, O Come, Emmanuel," which is taken from the final O Antiphon.

These poetic prayers reverberate with longing and hope. They tell us we need a rescuer and a ransom. They remind us that, even if we had never heard the name of Jesus, we would still need all he came to give. We need "wisdom, coming forth from the mouth of the Most High." We need Adonai—the Lord—to "come and redeem us with an outstretched arm." We need the root of Jesse to nourish us. We need the key of David to unlock the chains that imprison us. We need the rising dawn, "the radiance of the Light eternal and Sun of Justice." We need the king of the nations, the deepest "desire of all." And we need Immanuel, God with us.[5]

The O Antiphons remind us that the first coming of Christ should not be taken for granted, nor should its significance be consigned to the past. All the groaning of creation, all the tragedies and miseries of history, all the confusion and ignorance that characterized humanity before Christ remain with us now, even in the age of our Lord. There are billions of people today who, like those in the Old Testament, have never heard the story of Jesus. And we who have heard and believed the good news often find ourselves mired in fear, unbelief, sin, and sorrow. Because of this, we not only recall those who waited for Christ; we join with them each year to tell of the one who answers the yearning of every human heart and the desire of every nation.

The longing of Advent begins in the first pages of the Bible. In Genesis we watch with horror as sin enters the world through the rebellion of Adam and Eve. Poison is poured into the stream of humanity and death breaks loose on the earth. The wreckage is devastating and pervasive. Because of the fall there is brokenness in our bodies, in our interior lives, in our relationships with each other, in nature, in culture, and in societal systems. Our desires have become disordered and discordant, and we are now at odds with others and with God himself.

Then, in Genesis 3:15, there is the first whisper of hope:

> I will put enmity
>> between you and the woman,
>> and between your offspring and hers;

> he will crush your head,
>> and you will strike his heel.

Theologians calls this the *protevangelion*, the first gospel, which foreshadows the good news to come. It is the first hint that, though everything seems shattered beyond repair, God has not left us. Help is on the way. Generation after generation, through the promises of Abraham, the enslavement of the Jewish people, the deliverance of the exodus, through prophets and psalms, through the establishment and destruction of the temple, through exile and return, the people of God waited for God's anointed.

Slowly—painfully slowly—promises were unveiled to God's people of one who was coming whose kingdom would have no end. And slowly the people of Israel realized that these promises were not only for their own rescue but for all nations, ethnicities, and people groups. They waited and hoped, not knowing what was to come, unable to skip to the end of the book, unable to see what lay ahead.

Advent is a time to ready ourselves for the celebration of the incarnation, and this is no small task. The way we celebrate Christmas can easily become sentimental and trite. We are so familiar with the story—the little lambs

and the shepherds, the Christmas star and the stockings—
that we fail to notice the depth of pain, chaos, and danger
of the world into which Jesus was born.[6] Christmas with
its compulsory jollification and insistence on being the
"hap-hap-happiest season of all" devolves into saccharine
escapism if we do not first take note of the darkness in the
world and in our own lives.

Part of why we observe Advent is to make Christmas
weird again, to allow the shock of the incarnation to take
us aback once more. The movie *Talladega Nights* has a
famous scene in which Will Ferrell's character prays to the
"eight-pound, six-ounce, newborn infant Jesus." It's his "favorite Jesus." This kind of laughable mawkishness springs
from our casual overfamiliarity with the Christmas story
divorced from the larger story of the fall of the world and
God's redemption through Israel.

We rush too quickly to carols and bells and a sweet little
"eight-pound, six-ounce, newborn infant Jesus" and lose
sight of Jesus as the long-awaited Messiah—the one who
is wisdom, Adonai, root, key, light, king, and Immanuel.

By entering into the larger story of redemptive history,
we begin to feel our need of a deliverer again. We wipe
away the fake snow and tinsel, the felt-board shepherds

and friendly beasts, and lean into the ache of the cosmos, the sorrow and struggle of all creation.

Just as we are tempted to skip over the devastation of Good Friday and rush ahead to the good news of Easter, we can hurry to the hope of the incarnation and refuse to glimpse the depth of confusion and pain of the oppressed people of Israel, longing for God's shalom in a world devoid of peace. But in the same way that ignoring the horror of the cross inevitably belittles the resurrection, when we overlook the captivity and yearning of Israel, we end up missing the glory of that holy night in Bethlehem.

In the church calendar, every season of celebration is preceded by a season of preparation. In Advent, we prepare our hearts, minds, and bodies to receive the good news that awaits us in the twelve days of Christmas.

I did not grow up observing Advent—I didn't even really know what it was. Like many Americans, my family began celebrating Christmas the day after Thanksgiving. When I started attending an Anglican church in my late twenties, Advent drew me in. With its quiet beauty and doleful hymns, this season made intuitive emotional sense to me. Before we celebrate the birth of Christ, we remember the pain of labor—we wait with this whole longing world, with all of creation, groaning for redemption to be born. We face the darkness before we celebrate the dawn.

We prepare for Christmas not only with shopping lists and decorations but by making space for mourning. We join with Israel in lamentation. We wait, as the hymn says, "in lowly exile here, until the Son of God appears."

THE COMING OF CHRIST IN THE PRESENT

In John 14 Jesus tells the disciples that soon he will be going away, but he will not leave them as orphans. He will send the Holy Spirit, the "comforter" or "advocate" who will testify to the truth of everything Jesus has told them.

At Pentecost this promise is fulfilled. The people of God become the church, adopted as brothers and sisters into a new global family. Today we in the church continue to live in the same Spirit that shocked the disciples and the watching world at Pentecost. "The 'distance' between Peter-the-Disciple and Peter-the-Apostle is far greater than that between Peter and us," writes theologian Michael Horton. "After all, Peter-the-Apostle lived on this side of 'these last days,' as do we." Horton says a child can now recognize "Jesus in his saving office more fully than did Jesus' own brothers during his earthly ministry. This is because we live with the Apostle Peter on this side of Pentecost, where the age that Jesus inaugurated is at work, disrupting the powers and principalities that keep us from recognizing him."[7]

Pentecost gets its own liturgical season, but here in Advent we recall the hope it represents because we look for the coming of Christ not only in the incarnation but in our daily lives. Jesus came to us in the incarnation, but his work continues in us, through us, and all around us.

In Advent we take time to reflect on how Jesus, whom the people of Israel longed for, meets us today. We look at the places in our own lives where we yearn for Christ to come, places where we need hope, encouragement, help, and deliverance.

In Advent we also notice how Christ continues his work in the world. In years that feel full of turmoil—times where political strife, war, and global suffering dominate the news—I find myself hungry for Advent. In 2020, during the first year of the Covid-19 pandemic, I could not wait for Advent to begin. I needed it. I needed a time when we as a church could grieve the pain and sin in the world and wait for Christ to come, even now.

Advent is the season when we practice watching for grace. It is a time when we pay extra attention to how Christ continues to come, how he enters into the darkest corners of humanity and of our own lives. It is a time when we invite Christ to meet us and, in the words of Rich Mullins, to "shake us forward and shake us free."[8]

Advent is also the time when we recall that Christ comes to us actually and tangibly through the means of grace: through the Scriptures, through baptism, and through the Lord's Supper (or the Eucharist). That these are called the *means* of grace reminds us that grace is not a free-floating force, much less a warm, spiritual feeling, untethered from the earth and human history. Instead, grace is the reality that God is at work. And his work is most often through earthy things. These means of grace are the reliable ways in which we know Christ in the present. They are sturdy crags, handholds that allow us to continue in the way of Christ and offer us the presence of Christ, week in and week out.

Christ came to us in the incarnation, and he keeps coming to us through the Spirit. We are buried with him and raised with him in baptism (see Romans 6:3-4), washed in the water of regeneration (see Titus 3:5). We are given bread from heaven (see John 6:32) and his body and blood through the Eucharist (see 1 Corinthians 10:16). We receive the Word through his word, read and preached in the church.

We begin our year not only by waiting but by readying ourselves to receive the gifts of repentance, healing, and restoration that God gives by grace. We come to God openhanded, holding our imperfect and incomplete lives before him. We need him to come to us, to rescue and restore us, even today, in our everyday lives.

The Final Coming of Christ

"Christ has died. Christ has risen. Christ will come again."[9]

Every week at our church we say these mysterious words (called the "memorial acclamation") just before we receive the Eucharist. These words are what N. T. Wright has called a "portable story"—a short statement that sums up the larger narrative of the Christian faith.[10]

"Christ will come again." With these words we recall the third way we wait for Christ's coming in Advent.

Amid the familiarity and decorum of our weekly worship service, the strangeness of what we are proclaiming can be lost. But this is mind-boggling, imagination-bending stuff. We wait for Jesus to return, as John of Patmos has it, on "a white horse, whose rider is called Faithful and True," the armies of heaven following him, a sharp sword "coming out of his mouth" to judge the nations, and a robe inscribed "KING OF KINGS AND LORD OF LORDS" (Revelation 19:11-16).

In her book *Advent: The Once and Future Coming of Jesus Christ*, Fleming Rutledge says the *adventus glorificamus*, or Christ's coming in glory, is the chief and most important focus of Advent. It's also the primary focus of Advent throughout church history. Through this season we join with the whole historic and global church in waiting for Christ to come and finally set all things right.

When I first began to practice Advent, my focus was almost entirely on preparing for Christmas. I was surprised to discover, however, that Advent is uncomfortably and unavoidably apocalyptic, more concerned with a vast cosmic battle than dashing through the snow in a one-horse open sleigh. In late December, this preoccupation with the world to come can feel bizarre, if not downright Scroogey.

But waiting for Jesus' final return tinges the whole of Advent. Few of the Scripture readings and prayers in

Anglican Advent services are about the nativity (only in the fourth week do we set our sights on the annunciation and Mary's Magnificat). Again and again the actual experience of Advent in my church community, and in particular the Scripture readings I heard each Sunday, reminded me that this season is mostly about the end of this present age and the beginning of another. It is about the birth of "a new heaven and a new earth" (Isaiah 65:17-25; 2 Peter 3:13; Revelation 21:1). "Advent . . . differs from the other seasons in that it looks beyond history altogether," writes Rutledge. "In the cycle of the seasons and festival days that takes the church through the life of Christ, it is Advent that gives us the final consummation; it is the season of the last things."[11]

Jesus is coming, this time not as a vulnerable baby but as a powerful and conquering king, a merciful and just judge, to subdue sin and death and to birth a new world. Death will be undone. Tears will be wiped away. The tree of life, whose leaves will bring "the healing of the nations" (Revelation 22:2), will be the divine answer to the tree that brought destruction in the first pages of Genesis. Humanity will dwell again with God in a restored Eden.

This is very good news. At least it ought to be. Yet at times Christians have made the return of Christ seem either hokey or horrifying. In much of the popular media surrounding the "rapture" and the "apocalypse"—books, films, tracts, and so on—teachings about the *eschaton*, or the end times, are used as a scare tactic: give your life to Jesus or you'll have to endure catastrophes to come. When I think of the second coming of Christ, my mind flits between Tim Lahaye's Left Behind series, Hal Lindsey's *The Late Great Planet Earth*, and bumper stickers that proclaim, "In case of rapture, this car will be unmanned." My husband's childhood church in Georgia had an in-case-of-rapture vault (no joke) that contained a TV, a VCR, and a video explanation of what to do after the rapture had occurred and you were left behind. I suppose they hoped someone would stumble in and find it amid the apocalypse.

Churches with rapture vaults would be incomprehensible to the vast majority of Christians throughout time. The idea of the rapture as it's popularly conceived sprung up around the nineteenth century.[12] But as a child and a teenager, my husband didn't know this had not always been the church's teaching about Scripture. These ideas were in part why he gave up on church for a while after he left home for college.

These bizarre teachings are not good news. Bad second-coming theology has done a number on our theological imaginations. It has made the return of Christ seem like the stuff of badly written fan fiction, apocalyptic horror, and anti-intellectual pie-in-the-sky escapism. These novel teachings have made many Christians anxious about a doctrine that has historically been a chief source of hope for the church. In order to faithfully and fully enter into this "coming" of Advent, then, we may have some unlearning to do.

We Christians believe that Christ will, as the Nicene Creed says, "come again in glory to judge the living and the dead and his kingdom will have no end." This is God's definitive response to the deepest longings of the human soul. It is our hope that truth, beauty, and goodness will last, and that evil, sorrow, and death will not. It is the promise that we and all of the cosmos are not doomed to fate and left on our own, but that we will be made whole and new.

Advent, ultimately, is a season of hope, which is why it is mostly about Christ coming in glory. This is the truest object of our hope. We celebrate that Jesus came in his incarnation and find comfort in how he comes to us in our daily lives, but all of our longings meet their end in Christ coming again, bringing healing, peace, joy, and an unimaginable wholeness in his wake. The final return of Christ is the undoing of cancer. It is the utter dismantling of white supremacy and racism. It is the delivery of justice for the victimized, for the weakest and the most vulnerable whom the powerful have brutalized with seeming impunity. It is the regeneration of dead coral reefs. It is the end of global pandemics. It is the vindication of those falsely imprisoned. It is the weeping of children giving way to their eternal laughter. It is the death of death.

This hope utterly changes our relationship with the present. It is not that our life today does not matter. The relationships we make, the people we are becoming, the worship we render is eternal, and that reality lends depth and meaning to our lives in the present tense. But Advent reminds us that awaiting the final coming of Jesus is—and has always been—the essential posture of every Christian. No matter how sophisticated our technology or how privileged our lives, the Christian faith tells us that what we most long for is not to be found till the end of time.

In the resurrection of Jesus, we see the first evidence that the whole world will be made new. For now we live between Christ's finished work on the cross and his finished work on the throne. Things are not new yet. There is much pain and agony in this "time between the times." The world is a dark place. We can and must seek light, pursue justice, and agitate for change. This is part of the call of the church. Yet we must also acknowledge that any good we achieve, any justice we secure, is always partial and provisional. It is always, as Steve Garber says, "proximate justice."[13] Ultimately, this weary world waits for the world to come. The good news we look forward to in Advent, then, as Catholic priest Charles Riepe says, is "Jesus' glorious coming to complete his Easter work." So critical is this aspect of our faith that "the church goes so far as to set aside an entire liturgical season to the end of the world and the final coming of the Lord."[14]

We begin each Christian year looking ahead beyond time itself. We begin each year asking, "Will this be the year of Christ's coming?"

LIVING THE THREE ADVENTS OF CHRIST

Advent collapses time. The past, present, and future join together in a single season of waiting for Immanuel, God With Us.

There are two ways of talking about time in the Greek language in which the New Testament was written. One is *chronos*. This refers to the succession of time as we experience it, one linear moment after the next. *Chronos* is time that can be measured and kept in weeks, days, hours, and seconds. The other is *kairos*. This is the "fullness of time." This is the time of eternity. *Kairos* time marks the watersheds in human history and in our lives—moments that feel outside of time.

Advent happens in *chronos*, but, like all liturgical seasons, it steps into *kairos*. The whole church calendar—but especially Advent, with its three comings—is the interweaving of *kairos* and *chronos*. Past, present, and future are all equally present to us in this season. We wait with Israel in the past, we wait for Christ in the present, and we wait for his final coming in the future. Through *kairos*, Advent teaches us to enter into *chronos* as a different kind of people.

My yearly practice of waiting on these three comings of Christ shows me that I often forget how to wait on the Lord. I begin to believe I am the master and maker of my own life. I begin to believe that joy is self-made through my own ingenuity and hard work. I begin to believe that the things I most long for are within my grasp if I can only master the mad task of controlling my own life. I begin to believe I am the engineer of my own deliverance. And into these fevered deceptions, Advent comes each year and quietly asks me to pause, to remember that we do not bring the kingdom of God to the world through our own effort or on our own timeline. We wait for one outside of us and outside of time. We wait for our coming king.

2

Longing

FOUR THEMES OF ADVENT

The origins of Advent are shrouded in obscurity. The feast of the incarnation, which we now call "Christmas," is cited in writings from as early as the second century. But because it emerged organically in different places at different times, there was no set day for its celebration. The first time we see Christmas dated to December 25 is the year 336 in an almanac called the *Chronograph*, though it must have been widely celebrated on that day before then since it is mentioned as common knowledge.[1]

In these early mentions of Christmas, there is no evidence that it is preceded by a period of fasting and preparation like Advent. Easter was the first major feast of the church. In preparation for it, Christians began to practice Lent by the second century at the latest.[2] So as a parallel to Lent-Easter, Advent began to be widely observed before Christmas in the fourth century.[3] A pattern was established: fasts precede feasts. The final shape that we now associate with Advent came about much later, in the seventh century, as liturgical books called *Ordines Romani* began to provide details about how the Roman Mass was to be celebrated. These books establish a pattern for Advent, marking it as the four Sundays leading up to Christmas, with set readings, recited prayers, and hymns, and this remains roughly the way liturgical churches mark Advent to the present day.[4]

Unlike the Scripture readings, prayers, and songs of Advent, the themes of Advent are not straightforwardly appointed or recorded. Instead they emerge from the theology, worship, purpose, and history of this season. Nonetheless, as we spend time year after year keeping Advent, we slowly catch its tone and emotional tenor. We pick up on its vibe, on its emphases and priorities, on how it shapes our time and our faith, on the way its light falls across our lives.

WAITING AND HOPE

"Advent is a season for waiting," writes Bobby Gross in his book *Living the Christian Year*. "We wait for the coming of God. We need him to come. Our world is messed up, and we are messed up. We lament our condition and long for God to set things right, to make us better. So we pray and watch."[5]

But what does our waiting look like?

One of my family's most-watched movies is *Zootopia*. There's a scene in it where we find that the DMV of Zootopia is staffed entirely by sloths—all, of course, moving agonizingly slowly. The first time we saw it, all the adults in the theater cackled. We had all felt the frustration of long waits in bureaucratic offices.

At times it feels our lives are like the waiting room of a DMV run by sloths. Waiting feels sterile, dreary, depressing, and pointless. What we are waiting for is not worth the trouble and the boredom we are enduring. And the thought grows in us: What if those in charge—the ones making us wait—are incompetent? Or, worse, what if they get a kind of perverse joy in making the process as painful as possible? Or what if all this waiting just leads to more waiting? What if we are waiting for something that will never come?

A key part of Christian discipleship is to learn to wait with hope. The church is to be a people, Paul tells us, characterized by faith, hope, and love (see 1 Corinthians 13:13).

He says the greatest of these is love. But why? Faith will eventually become sight. Hope will eventually meet its object. In eternity, we will no longer need these particular virtues. They are like maternity clothes. Once eternity is born in us (or rather when we are born into eternity), we no longer need them. Love alone lasts. Faith and hope then are *waiting virtues*, which is precisely why we need them so desperately in the here and now. Practicing the church calendar is training in how to wait amid the pain of our lives and the tragedies of history with faith, hope, and love.

In Hebrews 11 we're presented with a litany of saints who act "by faith." The phrase "by faith" is repeated again and again throughout the chapter. Through it we glimpse what faith looks like. Faith is wagering our lives on the hope that we have, trusting it enough to act on it.

Faith and hope together form a kind of joyful expectancy. This is not the bored waiting at the DMV. It is a kid waiting for Christmas morning. A mother waiting for her child to be born. A weary worker waiting for an upcoming vacation. Patience, in turn, is not stoicism or resignation. It is instead the ability to look forward to and count on the greater good ahead.

Advent is marked by intense anticipation. We feel this in our liturgy and rituals. We light candles week by week till at last—at last!—Christmas arrives and we light the Christ candle. We celebrate that Immanuel has come.

This anticipation of Christmas, for us, isn't only a countdown to a big day of fun, feasts, and presents (though it is that), but it is a disposition that marks the whole Christian life.

Advent is a way to practice faith-and-hope-formed waiting. It's a way to begin the year explicitly foregrounding not our own plans, goals, success, or achievements, but the destiny God has written for his creation and for all humanity. We begin by recalling that we are merely creatures and by entrusting ourselves to the triune God, the protagonist of all of history and of time itself. He is the center of creation and the fulcrum of eternity. Through our corporate waiting in Advent, we slowly learn that our lives find their meaning in God's larger story of redemption and ransom of the whole cosmos.

Advent is a season of hope, but hope is not to be confused with privilege, peppiness, or a denial of just how broken things really are. We cannot embrace true hope without also acknowledging the pain and sinfulness of the world and of our own lives. Hope is the comfort of the poor and the needy. It is not a trite bliss formed through our own effort, wealth, or success.

Hope is also not mere optimism. Lesslie Newbigin famously said, "I am neither an optimist nor a pessimist. Jesus Christ is risen from the dead."[6] Christian hope is not a "whistling in the dark," a way to minimize the stark facts of reality. It is a conviction about the *ultimate* outcome of history, which is not in jeopardy: Jesus Christ has conquered sin and death.

During World War II, the Serbian bishop Nikolai Velimirovic was imprisoned at the concentration camp at Dachau. From there he wrote some of the most beautiful prayer-poems ever produced, later published as Prayers by the Lake. In one he writes, "Do not grumble against Heaven because it does not fulfill all your hopes. Grumble against yourselves because you do not know how to hope. Heaven does not fulfill hopes but hope. The most sublime and steadfast hope Heaven always fulfills."[7] Nikolai here rebukes the *smallness* of our hopes, the naive confusion of our "hopes" with the "most sublime and steadfast hope" found in Jesus alone. Entering faithfully into Advent helps wean us off our little hopes, our false hopes, and teaches us to place our confidence in the true hope of the world.

DARKNESS AND LIGHT

"The light shines in the darkness, and the darkness has not overcome it" (John 1:5).

John's Gospel is characterized by the contrast between darkness and light. Darkness is the realm of brokenness, sin, and deception, associated with guilt, shame, and hiddenness. Light banishes darkness, exposing what has been done in secret. Light *reveals*—which can be both terrifying and comforting. The larger context around the most well-known verse in the Bible, John 3:16, makes this clear. As verse 17 tells us, Jesus did not come to condemn the world but to save it; nonetheless, "this is the verdict: Light has come into the world, but people loved darkness instead of light because their deeds were evil. Everyone who does evil hates the light, and will not come into the light for fear that their deeds will be exposed" (John 3:19-20).

For those of us in the Northern Hemisphere, Advent is literally a dark time. Each night the hours of darkness stretch longer. There is an innate and deeply human fear of encroaching darkness and a longing for light to return.[8]

This is in part why there are so many pagan festivals that focus on darkness, light, and the winter solstice. The church uses the almost universal language of darkness and light to talk about the coming of Jesus. We wait in deepest darkness for the light of the world to come.

At Christmas, we celebrate how light entered into darkness. But first, Advent bids us to pause and look, with complete honesty, at the darkness. Advent asks us to name what is dark in the world and in our own lives and to invite the light of Christ into each shadowy corner. To practice Advent is to lean into a cosmic ache: our deep, wordless desire for things to be made right. We dwell in a world shrouded in sin, conflict, violence, and oppression. Christians must be honest about the whole of life—both death and resurrection, both the darkness and the light.

In Advent we take time to examine what is hidden. This season asks us to come clean about those things done in darkness. So many of the destructive things in our lives and in the world are shrouded in secrecy and shame—from human trafficking to porn addiction, from sweatshops to whispered gossip, from physical abuse to unacknowledged alcoholism, from corruption of power to quiet despair. Advent tells us that the light of the world, in his kindness, demands that every hidden thing be unveiled. David Foster Wallace wrote, "The truth will set you free. But not until it is finished with you."[9] Advent tells us we cannot welcome the light of the world while hiding the truth of who we are. We cannot follow the light of the world while we hide in the dark.

Before the delight of Christmas, Advent invites us to a vulnerable place—a place of individual and communal confession where we honestly name unjust systems, cultural decay, sorrow, the sin of the world, and the sin in our own lives. Only by dwelling in that vulnerable place can we learn to profess true hope. Not a cheap hope, spun from falsehoods, half-truths, or denial, but a hope offered by the very light that darkness cannot overcome.

REPENTANCE AND REST

There are two Advent sermons preserved from a bishop in the fifth century named Maximus of Turin. In those sermons he describes Advent as the time of preparation for the birthday of the emperor or king.

Preparing for a beloved king's birthday is a time of anticipation and even excitement. Everyone is cleaning, scrubbing, decorating, baking, and chattering about what the coming celebration will be like. It's exciting, yet everyone is working hard to get things ready because we understand instinctively that coming before the king is sobering. It's a big deal. At Advent, we recall that our king is coming. This is a joy. But, Maximus reminds his congregants, it also means we will be called to account and our lives will be subjected to scrutiny.[10] The Advent season has historically been a penitential season, a "little Lent," a time to seek repentance, humility, and renewal.

In the first Anglican church I joined, my priest, Fr. Thomas, explained how the liturgical color purple, the color most often used in Advent (and Lent), means both repentance and royalty. "Why both?" I asked him. "Aren't those pretty different ideas?"

He replied that the purple link between royalty and repentance tells us, "The king is coming! Get ready!"

Recalling Jesus' kingship throws into sharp relief the ways we seek to build kingdoms for ourselves, the ways we are often disloyal subjects. We live in a world that is busy making false kings. We ourselves are busy making false kings. We want our own way and our own self-worship. And the true king is coming. Gulp. Get ready.

So before we barrel into the celebration of Christmas, we are invited into the gift of repentance.

The complex emotional timbre of Advent is summed up for me by the Eastern Orthodox concept of "bright sadness." This idea names the antinomy of what Saint John of Sinai called the "joy-grief of holy compunction."[11] It speaks to the tension of heartache steeped in hope.

The Scripture readings in Advent accentuate the contrast between the perfect purity of Christ and the brokenness of the world he came to purify, judge, and save.

In this season of bright sadness, we notice the ways that sin entangles us, the places in our lives and communities that resist bowing the knee to this coming king.

Another year has gone by and we still live in a world in need of mending. We still have sorrow. Women and children still find they are not safe. The strong still prey on the weak. Creation still groans. Humanity is still not what it should be.

We, too, as individuals are not as we should be. We, too, need mending. We have our own idols, addictions, pettiness, conceits, and deceits. We have given and received wounds. We carry dark memories and painful scars.

Yet repentance flows from the hope that while our sin is real, it is not the most real thing. And it does not have the final word.

Repentance (*metanoia* in Scripture) literally means "changing your mind" or "turning around." The prophet Isaiah intriguingly pairs repentance with rest: "In repentance and rest is your salvation" (Isaiah 30:15). These feel like strange bedfellows to me. When I think of repentance I think of rigor, discipline, hard work, and willpower. Rest feels more like an invitation to relax, take a breather, unwind. How can these go together?

The Catholic priest Remi Hoeckman has said that to repent is "to rethink everything from the ground up."[12] This definition hints at the way in which repentance and rest entwine. The call to repent is not a call to get busier, trying to jam more good works into an already over-crowded schedule, redoubling our efforts to "do better." It is a call to step back and pay attention. Not to remake oneself but to be remade. Reimagining everything from the ground up is a process. It takes time. It takes a miraculous amount of grace.

By turning from sin—those things in our lives that promise rest but offer only diminishment—we learn true rest; rest that comes, in the end, as a gift. To repent is to quit our own efforts to save ourselves and to slow down enough to allow God to transform who we are.

The monk John Climacus wrote, "Repentance is the daughter of hope and the refusal to despair."[13] Advent is the season of hope, and repentance is an active way of putting on that hope and refusing to despair.

EMPTINESS AND FILLING

In the creation story God fills what is empty. He fills the empty land with trees and plants. He fills the empty sky with the sun and moon. He fills the empty sea with swimming things. He fills the earth with life.

In the story of Jesus' birth, the dawn of new creation, God fills empty places again. In her Magnificat, Mary sings that God "has filled the hungry with good things but has sent the rich away empty" (Luke 1:53). In the Christmas story, empty wombs are filled. Empty skies are suddenly full of angels. Empty mangers are filled with the light of the world.

One of the ways the Scriptures get our attention is repetition. In repeating a phrase or a theme the biblical authors tell us, "Hey! Look at this! This is important!" One of the most important repeated themes in all of Scripture is the so-called creation mandate of Genesis 1:28, "Be fruitful, and multiply" (KJV). In the Bible, whenever God intervenes decisively in the course of history, that moment is signaled by a repetition of this phrase or this theme. The original command is repeated after Noah and his family emerge from the ark in Genesis 9. Later, God tells Israel they will be fruitful and multiply if they are faithful to the covenant (Leviticus 26:9; Deuteronomy 7:13). The opening of barren wombs is always a sign in Scripture that God is at work to rescue and redeem his people.[14] Though the blessing of birth and new life is literal, it is also given to us as a metaphor: to be fruitful is not just to have biological children but to be, as it were, pregnant with the things of God. Righteousness and justice are the progeny of those who are filled with God's presence.

Barrenness, by contrast, is understood in the Bible as part of the curse that is on humanity after the fall, part of the affliction of living in a world marked by disappointment and futility. The sorrow of humanity frustrated by sin is like a woman longing for children but unable to bear them.

The heartache of infertility is of course one many people still carry today, and certainly the American church with its overemphasis on biological family has often made this burden worse. There should be no stigma for those who experience infertility. But in order to understand this motif in the Bible, we must understand that for the biblical writers, physical barrenness symbolized that things were not as they should be.

It is not for nothing, then, that the story of Christmas is a story about the opening of wombs. First Elizabeth's, then Mary's.

The life of Jesus also ushers in a new and fuller understanding of what fruitfulness is. Through his life and teaching Jesus makes the metaphorical meaning of fruitfulness the central meaning. The fruitfulness he demonstrates is not the fruitfulness of procreation but of "bringing many sons and daughters to glory" (Hebrews 2:10). It is not that Jesus disparages or condemns marriage and the creation mandate (he actually affirms it in Matthew 19). But as the kingdom of God crashes into the world in the person of Christ, a surprising reversal takes place in which true fecundity—true abundance—is spiritualized. The birth that most matters is the spiritual birth "from above" (John 3:31). The ultimate filling Jesus brings is the Holy Spirit's filling of the church, which forms a new family born through baptism.[15]

The fullness we hope for is something we will not experience this side of eternity, and one of the chief purposes of Advent is to develop in us a craving for abundance, a taste for eternity.

As we prepare for Christmas, we recall that we cannot run from the emptiness in our lives. Instead we wait for it to be filled in the right time, in the right way.

When I feel the emptiness—the loneliness, meaninglessness, futility, and loss—present even in my very good life, I rush to fill it. Winds of emptiness echo in a hollow moment of my day, and I run to distraction. I stuff my waking moments with busyness, social media, words, work, and consumption. These can be cheap attempts at creating my own sense of fullness.

Advent recalls that the emptiness in the world and our own lives can't be sated with hurry, buying power, social media likes, fame, success, politics, or even religiosity. We wait with Mary, with Elizabeth, with all of creation, for our emptiness to be filled.

3

Crying Out

TWO PROPHETS OF ADVENT

By practicing the liturgical year, the church "does" the story of God, as the late evangelical theologian Robert Webber wrote—proclaiming it, enacting it, planting it deep in our hearts and minds.[1] Advent isn't named in Scripture, but the whole point of Advent is to get us into the Scriptures and get *them* into *us*. These ancient words are the sturdy beams that bear the weight of Advent's hope.

The church calendar is a way to walk through the story of Scripture each year. And Advent in particular invites us to pause, to reflect on the wonder of the promised Messiah, to be shaped by the long story of redemption.

In his book *After Virtue*, Alasdair MacIntyre writes that we can only answer the question "What am I to do?" if we can answer a prior question: "Of what story or stories do

I find myself a part?"[2] Advent calls us back to who we are by retelling us the story of which we are a part. It reminds us that we are a people marked by longing, exiled in a world of tears. But we are not abandoned. We are waiting for redemption—for a wholeness that has come yet is still coming, just over the horizon, just beyond our grasp, but rushing toward us minute by minute, day by day.

Immersing ourselves in a narrative communicates truth to us in ways mere cognition cannot. Stories get into our bones. As the philosopher James K. A. Smith puts it, a story "gets under our skin and lodges itself in our memories, becoming sedimented in the background of our consciousness."[3] This is the gift of the Christian calendar.

Part of how we get the story "into us" is through the public reading of Scripture in our gathered worship. Week by week we are told the story again; the story of creation, of Israel, of Jesus, and of the church. We are told the story from different vantages so that by paying attention we can steep our imaginations in the whole mystery of God's redemptive work. While there has been a great deal of tinkering over the centuries in the selection of biblical passages to be read during Advent, by and large the texts are thematically similar.

The Scottish theologian T. F. Torrance says the pre-history of Jesus given to us in the Scriptures—in the lives of the prophets and stories of God's chosen people—is the "womb of the incarnation."[4] Advent, very aptly then, begins in this womb. Two men in particular serve as our chief guides—our midwives, if you will—throughout this season.

Two towering figures dominate Advent's horizon: Isaiah and John the Baptist.

ISAIAH AND COSMIC RESCUE

Israel's Scriptures are divided into three parts: the Torah (the "Law" or "Teaching"), the Wisdom books, and the Prophets. In Advent we focus particularly on the Prophets. This is not only because they are the main source of direct prophecies about the coming Messiah but also because they intensify the pleading call heard throughout the Hebrew Scriptures: repent and give allegiance to Yahweh alone. In other words: the king is coming! Get ready!

In the Scripture readings appointed for Advent in most liturgical traditions, we return to Isaiah again and again. The New Testament does as well. Its writers cite Isaiah more than any other Old Testament book except for the

Psalms. The biblical scholar John F. A. Sawyer says that "around one hundred verses from forty-five of the sixty-six chapters of Isaiah are either quoted directly or clearly alluded to mainly in the Gospels (forty-six), Paul (thirty) and Revelation (thirty)."[5] All told, there are over four hundred references to Isaiah in the New Testament, more than one per page in a typical three-hundred-page translation of the New Testament.[6]

The New Testament is so profoundly shaped by the vision of Isaiah that the early church referred to it as "the fifth Gospel." In the introduction to his fifth-century Latin translation of the Scriptures (called the Vulgate), Jerome wrote that Isaiah "should be called an evangelist rather than a prophet because he describes all the mysteries of Christ and the church so clearly that you would think he is composing a history of what has already happened rather than prophesying about what is to come."[7]

Christians understand Isaiah's prophecies as culminating in Jesus, the Messiah. Reading the promises of Isaiah together each Advent teaches us then to see the Scriptures not as a tangled mass of self-contradictory and confusing texts but as a single, unified story—with God as its primary author—that finds its coherence in and through the person of Jesus.[8] Isaiah's prophecies ask us to yearn with the people of God for the coming of the king. Whatever Isaiah thought, imagined, or intended as he wrote, the providential guidance of God has been to bring his words into relationship with Jesus. These Advent readings preach Christ in and through the Old Testament.

Isaiah also trains us to pay attention to textures of salvation and deliverance that we are not accustomed to noticing. Americans, including American Christians, tend toward rugged individualism. We tend to understand salvation as a purely individual event. Each of us individually "gets saved." This isn't entirely wrong, but it is incomplete—so incomplete that it distorts our understanding of the gospel. Isaiah's prophecies draw us into a more expansive vision of salvation, one that encompasses whole nations and peoples, indeed the whole of creation itself.

Of the twelve Old Testament readings appointed in the Book of Common Prayer for the three-year cycle of Advent readings, seven come from Isaiah's prophecies. Isaiah 2:1-5 envisions "the mountain of the LORD," a way of referencing Jerusalem and Mount Zion specifically, the high hill on the southeast side of the city on which David built a citadel and on which the temple was built. This, he says, is the site of the redemption of the nations.

Long before Isaiah, as the people of Israel were poised to cross over the Jordan into the Promised Land, Moses told them they needed to put into practice the commands of God so the nations surrounding Israel would see their wisdom and understanding and say, "'Surely this great nation is a wise and understanding people.' What other nation is so great as to have their gods near them the way the LORD our God is near us whenever we pray to him? And what other nation is so great as to have such righteous decrees and laws as this body of laws I am setting before you today?" (Deuteronomy 4:6-8).

Of course, we know how the story goes—despite being God's chosen people, Israel disobeys God's commands. She forgets her story. She forgets who she is. But in Isaiah's vision, Moses' instructions from Deuteronomy are fulfilled. The law goes out like a beacon from Zion and speaks to the hearts of the nations, and the nations say:

> Come, let us go up to the mountain of the LORD,
>   to the temple of the God of Jacob.
> He will teach us his ways,
>   so that we may walk in his paths. (Isaiah 2:3)

They also "beat their swords into plowshares" (Isaiah 2:4) and embrace the peace that they were made for.

Among a particular people in the particular land of Israel, the redemption of God takes root. It blossoms to encompass all the nations of the earth. The theme of the nations streaming to Israel is repeated in the readings from Isaiah for Advent (see Isaiah 11:10-16; 35:8-10).[9] One idea persistently sounded in the New Testament is that in Christ the nations have been granted "intimacy" with the God of Israel, "grafted in" to Israel rather than superseding it or leaving it behind, and sharing in its hopes (see Romans 9–11).[10] This is a picture of the salvation of Jesus: all nations communing with the God of Israel, learning from his wisdom, laying down their swords against one another. What's promised is not merely individual salvation but a global, multiethnic, and communal restoration and rescue. The fulfillment of this promise occurs even in the story of the nativity as the nations—represented by the Magi—bring their gifts to Jesus (Luke 2:1-19).

Isaiah's prophecies also brim with organic imagery. They envision a flourishing planet where deserts bloom (Isaiah 35:1-2). The Anglican biblical scholar Richard

Bauckham calls the visions of Isaiah an "ecotopia" in which humans dwell in harmony with animals and predator and prey are at peace with one another:[11]

> The wolf will live with the lamb,
>> the leopard will lie down with the goat,
> the calf and the lion and the yearling together;
>> and a little child will lead them. (Isaiah 11:6)

In Isaiah 65:17, God promises to "create new heavens and a new earth." Here, another dimension of salvation shines through the prophecies of Isaiah: the healing of creation as a whole. Not only is the relationship between God and individuals repaired, not only is the violent breach between nations and ethnic groups healed, but a wounded creation itself is repaired.

Christians throughout church history have held to this broad vision of salvation, and it has informed the church's engagement in social and environmental action.

In one sermon John Wesley says that in the new heavens and the new earth, not only humanity but "the whole brute creation will then, undoubtedly, be restored, not only to the vigor, strength, and swiftness which they had at their creation, but to a far higher degree of each than they ever enjoyed. They will be restored, not only to that measure of understanding which they had in paradise, but to a degree of it as much higher than that, as the understanding of an elephant is beyond that of a worm."[12]

The fulfillment of Isaiah's prophecies expands our vision of all the Messiah came to do and accomplish—and implicitly points us to how we are meant to respond to that salvation. If Isaiah's vision is truly what Jesus accomplished, then social and ecological justice are an ongoing part of the fullness of his salvation and work. It was Isaiah's vision of a renewed creation that motivated the Clapham Sect, through the influence of William Wilberforce, to create the first Society for the Prevention of Cruelty to Animals and to help end the brutal blood sport of bear baiting in London.[13] The conservationist group A Rocha has been similarly guided in its approach by Isaiah's vision of ecotopia.[14] In contemporary American evangelicalism, our overly individualistic, spiritualized view of salvation is far too small—formed more by modernity and revivalism than by the radical hope offered by the Scriptures themselves. Yet Isaiah's voice bellows through the ages. He tells us that even now the God of Israel is bringing a more vast and comprehensive salvation than we dare imagine.

JOHN THE BAPTIST AND COSMIC JUSTICE

As Advent begins, the curtains open not on the birth of Jesus or on him teaching the crowds or performing miracles. Instead we find a strange figure in the desert—a long-haired, feral-looking ascetic who is announcing the kingdom of God and baptizing the pungent masses. John the Baptist takes center stage. "He is the herald of the age to come," writes Fleming Rutledge, "as prophesied by Malachi at the very end of the Old Testament."[15]

In Advent we seek to prepare the way of the Lord in the world and in our own lives—and there's no better guide than John the Baptizer. His outsized place in the typical Scripture readings of Advent is due to his role in preparing the way for Jesus. In explaining who John is, Jesus references a prophecy that Elijah, who was taken into heaven on a fiery chariot, would return to call Israel back to their true God. Then Jesus says Elijah has already returned in the person of John the Baptist, but Israel did not receive him but rather killed him, just as they would do to the Son of Man.

As the new Elijah, John sums up the entire prophetic tradition of the Old Testament, but he also looks forward to the new age of the Messiah. He straddles two worlds, calling down the judgment of God on the former age but also looking forward to the redemption of God in the age to come. In this liturgical season, which marks that liminal space on the cusp of the new era of the Messiah, John the Baptist dwells with us. John "is the last and greatest of the Hebrew prophets," writes Fleming Rutledge, "but far more important, he is the first person to belong to the arriving age of the kingdom of God."[16] Though John embodies the Old Testament prophets, he also stands in for us now. John not only announces the first coming of the Messiah; he also proclaims the ultimate judgment in the age to come.

John prefigures the prophetic role of Jesus by announcing that the reign of sin and death is coming to an end. He points us to the Messiah and also proclaims what is uncomfortably and inconveniently true: our hypocrisy, our wayward egos, our broken promises, our need for repentance. He does not mince words. He calls the Pharisees and Sadducees—ideologically opposed religious sects—a "brood of vipers" (Matthew 3:7). This would be analogous to denouncing both the political and religious left and right today. Jesus' pronouncement that at the end of the age everything hidden will be revealed (see Luke 8:17) is matched in certainty and intensity by the severe words John the Baptist speaks to the Pharisees and Sadducees: "The ax is already at the root of the trees, and every tree that does not produce good fruit will be cut down and thrown into the fire" (Matthew 3:10). He's not messing around.

John the Baptist is a political figure in the sense that he represents the judgment of God on all the oppressive, destructive, and nihilistic impulses of humanity. He and all God's prophets are threats to corrupt regimes and self-serving leaders who grasp power at the expense of others, which is why those in power so often see the prophets as dangers that need to be eradicated.

The brutality of John's unjust execution, the macabre image of his head on a platter held by the daughter of Herodias, reminds us what a threatening political figure John really was.[17] As Fleming Rutledge writes:

> When he appears on the banks of the Jordan, the cover-ups come to their appointed end. Two thousand years before all the Watergates, Irangates, and other sordid "-gates," John came proclaiming God's imminent judgment on the venality of governments, the corruption of police departments, the

greed of financiers, the selfishness of the rich, the self-righteousness of the religious establishment. . . .

There are cover-ups of all sorts. There are families that will not acknowledge the alcoholism that is destroying them. There are people who are making their loved ones miserable but will not go to a therapist. There are secretaries who cover up for bosses, business partners who cover up for each other, colonels for generals, bishops for clergy, parents for children. Advent is the season of the uncovering: "Bear fruit that befits repentance. . . . Even now the axe is laid to the root of the trees"! This is the right time to root out the cover-ups in our own lives, as we wait with bated breath for the lights to come on and the announcement of the angel that God is not against us but for us.[18]

John's starring role in Advent reminds us that this season is surprisingly and counterculturally political and ascetical. To heed his warning is to recognize that the problems with the world are not just "out there" among those supposed uniquely evil people—among our political or ideological enemies. They are inside us and spring from us as well. The line between good and evil runs through every human heart, as Aleksandr Solzhenitsyn reminds us,[19] and so we find John's steely gaze turned in our direction, reminding us that we too are part of systems of suffering in this world, that we make our own contribution to the misery of others, that we are victimizers as well as victims.

But we are not left without hope. We are called to repent and to remember soberly that Christ is coming again in glory, that we want to be counted among his friends and not his enemies. We are reminded that he sees and knows the ways the strong exploit the weak and will act on their behalf. We also must recall that although John shows God's determined opposition to sin and oppressive power, the Messiah for whom he prepared the way is— always and in every way—for us and not against us. It is the love of God, in the end, that wins the day. The love of God is the blazing fire that purifies us, remakes us, and sets right all that is broken in us and in the world. The love of God brings us to repentance. The love of God sets the oppressed free and makes all things new. The love of God insists on truth and justice. The love of God reveals every hidden thing. And it is this love that is coming for us.

4

Stirring

Like the whole of the Christian calendar, Advent intends to teach us how to pray—and, through prayer, how to believe.

There is an old saying in the church from the patristic theologian Prosper of Aquitaine: *Lex orandi statuat lex credendi*, "The law of prayer is the law of belief." What Prosper describes here is the mystery of formation. We all have preconceived, inherited, or invented notions of who or what God is. These float beneath the surface of our consciousness, usually unacknowledged, yet they drive who we are and what we do. God in his kindness accommodates himself to us and meets us where we are, even amid the half-cocked ideas, ill-formed impressions, and false notions of God that quietly roil our souls.

But also in his kindness, God works to heal our imaginations so that we might have a truer and more beautiful impression of who he actually is. This is in part why we need received and written prayers. The experience of coming to these prayers again and again, with our church community and as individuals, acts as a kind of medicine. The prayers the church has handed down generation to generation help rehabilitate and reshape our (often latent) views of God. In prayer we meet God as he is and, over time, this changes how we walk through the world and what we believe. The law of prayer is the law of belief.[1]

The liturgical scholar Aidan Kavanaugh points out that this is actually a shocking claim: "It implies that worship conceived is what gives rise to theological reflection, rather than the other way around."[2] We have to experience God in worship before we reflect on him. We do not start with an abstract, propositional knowledge of God and then create worship based on that image, but rather the worship of God in Word and sacrament gives shape and form to our theology. Of course, this isn't quite linear or straightforward. There is, we hope, a virtuous feedback loop at play in which doctrine and teaching—what we claim to believe about God—shape how we pray even while prayer shapes what we believe. But the point is this: to pray certain prayers is to be formed by those prayers. We are what we pray.

Liturgical churches have therefore given us prayers as a way to form Christians across time. In the Anglican tradition, the Book of Common Prayer collects some of these. It also appoints prayers for each week, including the four weeks of Advent. The appointed prayers from this collection are called the "collect" of the week.

The first prayer book imported about two-thirds of its collects from the medieval Latin Mass, and the rest were added as original compositions, most by the sixteenth century archbishop of Canterbury, Thomas Cranmer. These collects are, by and large, gorgeous. They are prayers, but they are also, in a loose sense, poetic. They make good use of words. They sing.

In early Anglicanism, these collects were revolutionary. They were ancient prayers that many were hearing in their own language (instead of Latin) for the first time.

The collects in most cases draw on and summarize the themes of the Scripture readings appointed for that week's worship service, so they also serve as a meditative summary of the Scriptures and themes of a liturgical season.[3]

In its prayers, Advent holds together preparation for the incarnation, meditation on the second coming in glory, and celebration of the means of grace given to sustain us in the meantime. The prayers of Advent are "meantime" prayers. They teach us to live in the crucible of the present moment, the time between the coming of the kingdom in Christ's ministry and the culmination of that kingdom in his coming judgment.

We do not grasp the hope of Advent primarily through thinking about Advent but instead through immersion into the practices and prayers of Advent. We prepare for the three comings of Christ by taking up Advent in an embodied way with an embodied congregation. And—as it has for Christians for millennia—this begins and ends with communal prayer.

The Collects of Advent

The Advent collects have been altered slowly over time. Originally, the season was mostly penitential in tone, mainly focused on preparation for Christ's final return

and judgment. But in the twentieth century that emphasis began to shift, largely through a close collaboration
between Anglican, Lutheran, Roman Catholic, and Orthodox liturgical scholars—a surprising work of Christian
unity.[4] Their work recasts the season of Advent to be
more balanced—both backward and forward facing.[5]

Still, the trippy, cosmic imagery in the Scripture
readings for Advent is drawn out and highlighted by the
collects, which invite us to "inwardly digest" these themes
as we pray together as a congregation. Again and again in
the typical liturgical Advent readings and collects we en-
counter the uncomfortable idea of God's judgment. There
is a starkness to the divine judgment that stands over all
human attempts to remake the world, to solve what is
wrong, and this theme of judgment looms large in the
Scripture readings of Advent. This is countercultural and
often distressing. Sit with Advent long enough and a
sense of our own helplessness to save ourselves will grow.

But more importantly, again and again in Advent we
collide with the idea of grace. A line that is repeated in
various ways throughout Saint Augustine's *Confessions* is,
"Grant what you command, and command what you will."[6]
Augustine understood that if we are going to live in

obedience to God, God himself must supply the capacity to do so. Grace not only offers forgiveness when we blow it; it transforms us into people who walk in the light. Grace gives us the unearned righteousness of Christ, but it also slowly sets us free from the anxiety, selfishness, apathy, and fear that burden our lives. And so throughout these collects, the emphasis falls less on our actions and more on the action of God teaching and empowering us to do as he has commanded.

Cast Away the Works of Darkness

> Almighty God, give us grace to cast away the works of darkness, and put on the armor of light, now in the time of this mortal life in which your Son Jesus Christ came to visit us in great humility; that in the last day, when he shall come again in his glorious majesty to judge both the living and the dead, we may rise to the life immortal; through him who lives and reigns with you and the Holy Spirit, one God, now and forever. Amen.[7]

In its contrast between "the works of darkness" and "the armor of light," the collect for the first Sunday in Advent alludes to Paul's language in Romans 13:8-14, a passage often read in liturgical churches on the first week in Advent. Part of it reads, "And do this, understanding the present time: The hour has already come for you to wake up from your slumber, because our salvation is nearer now than when we first believed. The night is nearly over; the day is almost here. So let us put aside the deeds of darkness and put on the armor of light" (Romans 13:11-12).

For Paul, the work of transformation—of casting off the works of darkness and putting on the armor of light— is urgent because of his understanding of "the present time." As Oliver O'Donovan notes, although we find calls for God to act throughout the Hebrew scriptures, there is no such petition anywhere in the New Testament. Rather, the New Testament assumes that God has already acted, and acted decisively. Instead we are the ones now summoned to wake up to what God has already done and is even now accomplishing.[8] God's work is soon to be completed. We eagerly await the coming of the Lord and, Paul reminds us, we are nearer to it now than when we first believed. We live under the assumption then that God is active in the world.

The time in which we are living is like the moments just before dawn, Paul says: "The night is nearly over; the day is almost here" (Romans 13:12). There is, as O'Donovan says, a "practical immediacy" to future redemption. We are readying ourselves to be engulfed by it. Paul is calling us to realize that even though Christ's coming is in the future, "it is also present, because it is now . . . that we confront it and may deliberate about it."[9] This is why elsewhere Paul says, "Now is the time of God's favor, now is the day of salvation" (2 Corinthians 6:2).

In this passage in Romans, Paul calls us to live in the daytime—the time when what we do is on full display, the time when nothing can be hidden in darkness. He calls the people of God away from living in "immorality and debauchery" and "dissension and jealousy" (Romans 13:13). In doing so, he equally condemns sins that are obvious, stigmatized, and clearly disreputable and those that are seemingly more common and "respectable." Both the deplorable degenerates and those who appear put together and upright are judged here, and both are found wanting. But all of us together are also offered grace.

The collect shifts between ages, recalling that all of our lives are lived between the age of this mortal life, in which sin and death still roar and reign (Romans 6:3-6), and the age of the last day, when the work Christ has done will be fully manifest—when he judges, as the Nicene Creed reminds us, the living and the dead. The two ages are characterized by strikingly different postures of Christ. This contrast was regularly highlighted and celebrated throughout history, and especially in the early church.

In the fourth century Cyril of Jerusalem preached a sermon to those who had converted to Christianity and were preparing for baptism. He described the two comings of Christ, drawing out parallels and differences. His words echo still today. This sermon sounds surprisingly contemporary because, in a real sense, Cyril lived in the same age we do. We were born millennia apart but we are both in the same generation of these "last days." We both live in this strange meantime—between the first and final comings of Christ. Across thousands of years we wait together, sharing the same hope. Cyril is still preaching to us:

> We preach not one advent only of Christ, but a second also, far more glorious than the former. For the former gave to view His patience; but the latter brings with it the crown of the divine kingdom. For all things, to speak generally, are twofold in our Lord Jesus Christ. . . . In His former advent, he was

wrapped in swaddling clothes in the manger; in His second, He covers Himself with light as with a garment. In His first coming, He endured the Cross, despising the shame; in His second, He comes attended by the Angel host, receiving glory. Let us not then rest in His first advent, but look also for His second. And as we have said at His first coming, Blessed is He that comes in the name of the Lord, so will we repeat the same at His second coming; that with the Angels, meeting our Master, we may worship him and say, *Blessed is He that comes in the Name of the Lord.* The Savior comes, not to be judged again, but to judge them who judged Him. . . . Then, he came by a divine disposition, teaching men with persuasion; but this time they will of necessity have Him for their King, though they wish it not.[10]

HEAR, READ, MARK, LEARN, AND INWARDLY DIGEST

Blessed Lord, who caused all Holy Scriptures to be written for our learning: Grant us so to hear them, read, mark, learn, and inwardly digest them, that by patience and the comfort of your holy Word we may embrace and ever hold fast the blessed hope of everlasting life, which you have given us in our Savior Jesus Christ; who lives and reigns with you and the Holy Spirit, one God, for ever and ever. Amen.

The second collect for Advent at first seems out of place. It appears to veer off in an entirely new direction. Here we are in the weeks leading up to Christmas, and then, out of the blue, the church pipes up about the goodness of the Bible. In this collect we thank God who "caused all Holy Scriptures to be written for our learning" and then ask for grace that we may "hear them, read, mark, learn, and inwardly digest them."

But if we look to the Scriptures that are typically appointed for this week of Advent, this prayer makes more sense. One passage often read is 2 Peter 3:3-4, where Peter exhorts his audience, "Above all, you must understand that in the last days scoffers will come, scoffing and following their own evil desires. They will say, 'Where is this "coming" he promised? Ever since our ancestors died, everything goes on as it has since the beginning of creation.'"

Here, Peter gestures to how difficult waiting with faith can be. We begin to wonder, *Is Jesus actually coming again? Is any of this stuff the church proclaims even true?*

Our problem, Peter says, is one of memory. Those who scoff "deliberately forget" (2 Peter 3:5) the story of Scripture. He reminds his hearers that time does not work for God like it works for us. Peter calls us to remember our story and hold fast to it, even if it feels like our waiting is long and hard. God seems to be moving slowly, but, Peter says, this isn't because he does not see us or does not care (Psalm 50:21). Instead, God's seeming slowness flows from his overflowing, bountiful love. God is profoundly *patient*, not wanting any to be lost (2 Peter 3:9). Peter tells us that only in keeping the word of God before our eyes and on our lips does it become the animating principle of our lives.

I struggle with this. Scripture often leaves me befuddled, frustrated, and uncertain. For me, holding to the truth of God's word is more like a wrestling match than an easy walk on a summer's day. Belief drains out of me like a sieve. It helps me to recall that hearing, believing, and obeying the word of God have never been easy and that striving to "enter through the narrow door" (Luke 13:24) has never felt more natural than it does now. Christians for thousands of years have had to work—*to read, mark, learn, and inwardly digest* the Scriptures—in order to believe and hold fast to the gospel. We aren't the first generation to struggle with unbelief. We will not be the last.

What Christians claim about the return of Christ is not obvious. It's weird. It can seem to contradict the evidence around us. And so Peter tells us that if we do not rehearse this story—reminding ourselves again and again that this is what we are waiting for and longing for—we will inevitably live by another story. We will cease to believe.

"I wish our hearts were already sighing with longing for that ineffable glory!" preached Saint Augustine. He believed we should be living our lives—"our pilgrimage"—not with love for the world, but "pushing out towards he who has called us." A life of longing and sighing will never comport with the promises of American consumerism, progress, or living our best life now. This will always feel difficult for us. It will always be a stretch. Yet this is the faithful Christian life, says Augustine. The church gathers each week to read the Scriptures together and celebrate the sacraments, not to satisfy our longings but to make them more acute, more aching, more intense. Augustine says the point of gathered worship—the point of hearing and receiving the word of God—is to "sow and germinate" our longing for more, to grow and expand it, so that it creates a space within our souls that only God can fill.[11]

Both Peter and Augustine see something crucial: love for and trust in God must be cultivated. It does not come naturally. Left on our own, our passions and cravings (Galatians 5:24; see also James 1:12-14; 4:4) point away from God to false gods. James K. A. Smith and others have highlighted the fact that in our secular age, the people we minister to and live among (even those in the church) often do not seem to have a "God-shaped hole" that needs to be filled, and we can be confused and distressed by this.[12] But Peter and Augustine recognized this long before us—it is natural for humans to worship *something*, but it is only by grace that we learn to worship what is real and true.

Grace reorients our desires toward God. This is a long, winding, and often uncomfortable process. And this reorientation, though always miraculous, comes to us in large part through ordinary, sometimes boring, means: the reading and preaching of the Scriptures, praying prayers, gathering with the church, and practicing the sacraments.

Part of what it means to wake up to what God has done in Jesus Christ is to wake up to what he is doing among us now through these ordinary means of grace. This prayer, then, recalls the Advent of Jesus in the present. Jesus comes to us in the means of grace, particularly—drawing on the reading from 2 Peter 3—in the reading and preaching of the Scriptures. As our imaginations are immersed in the story of the Scriptures—hearing, reading, marking, learning, and inwardly digesting them—the story of Jesus making all things new becomes the orienting and anchoring story of our lives. We learn to live in hope of a world to come. The Advent of Jesus, through these means of grace, allows us to continue to wrestle, to continue to believe, and to continue to wait for the promised Advent to come.

You Sent Your Messengers the Prophets

O Lord Jesus Christ, you sent your messengers the prophets to preach repentance and prepare the way for our salvation: Grant that the ministers and stewards of your mysteries may likewise make ready your way, by turning the hearts of the disobedient toward the wisdom of the just, that at your second coming to judge the world, we may be found a people acceptable in your sight; for with the Father and the Holy Spirit you live and reign, one God, now and for ever. Amen.

Ben Witherington III summarizes the work of the prophets as both "foretelling" and "forthtelling"—promising the coming of Christ and also "telling the truth about the believer's condition or about God's plans and promises."[13] The prophets "preach repentance" and "prepare the way for our salvation." They ready Israel for Christ's announcement and embodiment of the kingdom of God.

In this collect we trace the footsteps of those who've gone before us. We recall in particular the vocation of our Advent guides Isaiah and John the Baptist. Their mission was to announce both the coming judgment and the coming rescue. They were told to sound an alarm but also to offer comfort (see Isaiah 40:1).

This collect calls us in the church today to follow in those same footsteps. It turns out that the prophets' vocation and ours are not so different. We—the stewards of mysteries—are called to ready the way, "by turning the hearts of the disobedient toward the wisdom of the just." We too are called to prepare for the coming of Jesus.

Jon Cosin, the seventeenth-century Anglican bishop who wrote this collect, drew inspiration from a passage in

Matthew that is often read during Advent.[14] In it Jesus quotes a passage from the Old Testament book of Malachi:

> I will send my messenger ahead of you,
>> who will prepare your way before you.
>>> (Matthew 11:10; see also Malachi 3:1)

In a shocking twist, Jesus says the passage is about his cousin John the Baptist. John's true identity is revealed: he is a prophet pointing the way to Christ.

The church takes up this same identity. This collect highlights the prophetic character of our ministry—the continuing work of the people of God.

Here in the middle of Advent, just weeks before Christmas, we pray for ministers. The timing may seem strange. But it makes sense that at the beginning of the church calendar, at the start of a new year of ministry, we recall that both leaders and lay people in the church must continue the work of Isaiah and John. So we begin by acknowledging that we need help. If God commands that we too "prepare the way of the Lord," we need God's grace to grant what he commands.

What might it mean now for the church to be truly prophetic? How can we be an alternative community that follows Isaiah and John the Baptist in pointing others to Christ?

The theologian Stanley Hauerwas gave perhaps one of the shortest commencement addresses ever at the University of Aberdeen in 2017. Clocking in at less than five minutes long, the address focused on one idea: "Do not lie." Amid a world, a political system, a church, and a society full of untruth and half-truths, we must again take up the prophetic task of truth telling. We must be scrupulously and holistically honest about the world, ourselves, and God. This is what we see in the lives of the prophets. Hauerwas said that to endeavor not to lie requires us to live a life "at home in the truth."[15] In a culture where lying is rampant, where we instrumentalize relationships to our own ends, where we teem in self-justification and spin, where we minimize the faults of our own political and ideological tribe while exaggerating those of our opponents, where we share false information and gossip online and embrace conspiracy theories, the church must recover a radical commitment to knowing and proclaiming truth. "We don't lie," wrote theologian Will Willimon, reflecting on Hauerwas's address, "because it's our job to show that Jesus Christ makes possible lives of truth in a world of lies."[16]

STIR UP YOUR POWER, O LORD

Stir up your power, O Lord, and with great might come among us; and as we are sorely hindered by our sins from running the race that is set before us, let your bountiful grace and mercy speedily help and deliver us; through Jesus Christ our Lord, to whom, with you and the Holy Spirit, be honor and glory, now and for ever. Amen.

The Scripture readings in the final week of Advent, called Annunciation Sunday in the Book of Common Prayer, fix our eyes on the announcement of the incarnation by the angel Gabriel to Mary: "Do not be afraid, Mary; you have found favor with God. You will conceive and give birth to a son, and you are to call him Jesus. He will be great and will be called the Son of the Most High. The Lord God will give him the throne of his father David, and he will reign over Jacob's descendants forever; his kingdom will never end" (Luke 1:30-33).

This collect must be understood in context of the annunciation story. The Lord did indeed stir up his power and come among us through the very blood, bones, and womb of a young woman. With its focus on the annunciation, this fourth Sunday of Advent is a hinge in time. Mary sums up all the generations of preparation and waiting that came before her. As the church together waits in longing for the coming of Jesus, we remember two thousand years ago when one teenage girl, her belly swollen with life, waited to go into labor. Mary more than anyone else in Scripture embodies the vulnerability of joy and waiting.

The angel tells Mary that "the Holy Spirit will come on you, and the power of the Most High will overshadow you. So the holy one to be born will be called the Son of God" (Luke 1:35). Mary—young, alone, and (we assume) scared—responds with breathtaking faith. Her words echo down through the ages: "May your word to me be fulfilled" (Luke 1:38). Her trust and surrender to the wild and unpredictable will of God has been celebrated throughout Christian history.

The church historian Jaroslav Pelikan says that in this moment Mary acts as the paradigm showing us the way of life to which every believer aspires: to say "yes" to the work of God.[17] Mary—this humble, barely postpubescent girl, who was likely illiterate or semiliterate, with no wealth and no status, from a backwater town—matchlessly shows us what Christian faithfulness looks like. For that reason, as Mary says in the Magnificat, all generations shall call her blessed (Luke 1:48). And indeed all generations have, even among Protestants, who have tended to tone down the veneration given her.

Gerard Manley Hopkins wrote of the magnitude of what Mary did:

Mary Immaculate,
Merely a woman, yet
Whose presence, power is
Great as no goddess's
Was deemèd, dreamèd; who
This one work has to do—
Let all God's glory through. . . .
Gave God's infinity
Dwindled to infancy
Welcome in womb and breast,
birth, milk, and all the rest.[18]

But even as Mary's faith has rightly been celebrated across the Christian tradition, what most dominates her story is the theme of God's grace. The annunciation, along with Mary's faithful response to it, is part of a much larger divine drama in which she is only a bit player. Human action is significant, but it is "decentered" in the longer story of God that Advent represents. The protagonist in this story is always God, who opens wombs and turns the hearts of parents to their children and children to their parents[19] (see Malachi 4:6; Luke 1:17), who renews the face of the earth (see Psalm 104:30). As we meditate on the annunciation, it is, in the end, God who stands in the spotlight and captures our gaze.

In Luke, where Mary is more significant an actor than in other Gospels, she is nonetheless primarily a *recipient* of God's unearned favor. Her grateful response to Gabriel's news makes this clear. Twice in the second chapter of Luke's Gospel we hear that Mary "treasured" in her heart the things that were said to her (Luke 2:19, 51). Here Mary is in fact hearing, marking, learning, and inwardly digesting the "Scriptures" that were spoken to her, holding them close and meditating on them until they became the orienting story of her life.

In Greek, Mary's name is Μαριὰμ, which is the same name as Moses' and Aaron's sister in the Old Testament (typically translated as "Miriam"). After Yahweh humiliates the Egyptian gods through the ten plagues and delivers his people across the Red Sea, Miriam begins to sing and dance, reveling in Yahweh's love, power, and deliverance:

> Sing to the LORD,
>> for he is highly exalted.
> Both horse and driver
>> he has hurled into the sea. (Exodus 15:21)

Gabriel's promise to Mary is the ultimate vindication of Miriam's song.[20] The story of the annunciation is a declaration that God, in the life of Jesus, has begun a new and greater exodus out of sin and death (in Luke 9:31, Luke explicitly calls Jesus' death an *exodos*, often translated as "departure"). Mary's song, the Magnificat, echoes Miriam's. It is her joyful celebration of God's work of deliverance. Mary and Miriam are two women, generations apart, who sing together. They sing the same song of hope.

Mary is not mentioned in this collect, of course. But the focus of the fourth week of Advent—the announcement of God's power and rescue—reverberates through both this prayer and the story of Mary. Mary becomes "translucent" so that through her faithful action, God's love for the world in Jesus can become visible.[21] It is not the person of Mary who is centered in this collect but the content of her Magnificat and the ultimate object of her song.

We need God to come among us in his power. But when he does, we inevitably find that "we are sorely hindered by our sins from running the race that is set before us." What is there then left to do? We cry out for grace, for help, for deliverance.

The deliverance of God, our rescue from sin and death, can never be a half-measure. It must go down to the very roots—it must destroy the chief tyrants of this age: sin, death, and the devil.[22] Only by doing so can the "pervasive depravity"[23] in all of us be healed. The Magnificat, Mary's song on which we meditate on this hinge Sunday, and this collect, which summarizes it, call us to a more profound awareness of the effects of sin so that we are also more profoundly filled with longing for God's deliverance of all the world, including even ourselves.

5

Approaching

EIGHT PRACTICES OF ADVENT

When people find out you're writing a book on Advent, they inevitably ask the same question: How soon is it okay to start listening to Christmas music?[1]

So I need to be upfront and tell you: I am not going to answer that question directly. Sorry to disappoint you.

I'm not providing a fixed date to crank up your favorite Christmas album because there is no clear right answer. There is an honest tension between our desire to keep Advent and our culture's celebration of Christmas (including those churches that don't observe liturgical time), which seems to creep earlier and earlier in the calendar each year.

The two observances seem to pull in different directions. The holidays in America are marked by mass consumption. Stuff, stuff, and more stuff. But Advent tells us that wealth and possessions are not our rescuer. We cannot find salvation through buying power. Instead we wait for restoration and redemption.

American Yuletide celebrations insist on revelry and at times debauchery. Advent calls us to reflection, repentance, and at times self-denial. The holiday season with its crowds and festivities moves at warp speed. I have to rush just to keep up. But Advent asks us to decelerate, be still, and rest.

Advent then is unavoidably countercultural. It gives us a chance to remember every year that we are called to be a different sort of people. We are strangers and aliens. Christians always have been and always will be a people who are never quite at home in the world. The worst moments in church history have come when the church sought to be a power broker in culture or when it capitulated in cowardice to the norms of the broader culture. This offers a repulsive Christian witness that fails to represent the truly radical and shocking kingdom of God.

In a teeny-tiny, noncombative yet still subversive way, Advent reminds us that to follow Christ is always to be a misfit. It's training wheels for discipleship. Through Advent we see that being a misfit may not always be easy or uncomplicated, but it is always the call of Christ to his church.

The tricky part of being countercultural, however, is to figure out how to do so graciously, without being a crank, a grinch, or an obnoxious jerk. One of the hardest things about Advent is how to honor it as a season of preparation and penance without being a total killjoy as Christmas bells ring around us.

Advent is a gift from the Christian tradition, not a burden to be wearily shouldered or a perch from which to look down on holiday revelers. As with the rest of the church calendar, keeping Advent is a helpful and formative spiritual practice, but it is not a command. Spiritual director and author Jared Patrick Boyd often reminds us that we need to understand spiritual practices as invitations.[2] When we hear or learn about them, we need not receive them as another brick atop our already heavy load, another task to clutter our to-do list. Instead we ask, What is God's invitation to me through this discipline and in this season of my life?

These practices of Advent then are a gracious invitation rather than a checklist. There is no requirement to do all of them. The point of all Christian practices—from gathered worship to prayer to the liturgical calendar—is, as Hebrews 10:24 says, to stir us up "toward love and good deeds." As disappointing as it may be for some of us overachievers, no one is grading us on Advent. There is no Advent honor roll. And this is why the most important question about Advent is not how to get it all right, but whether it's stirring up love and good deeds in us.

Whether you wait till Christmas Eve to decorate your tree or trot out your loudest Christmas sweaters the day after Thanksgiving, the call of Advent is to follow Jesus in joy, gentleness, kindness, and hope. Advent doesn't wag its finger, bah-humbugging any hint of joy that raises its holly-decked head before December 25. Instead the ancient church offers us an invitation.

The traditions of Christians in generations before us and the global disciplines of the church help us learn to keep Advent with grace. Eugene Peterson writes that the Anglican priest Martin Thornton would read spiritual books and impatiently scrawl in the margins "YBH"— "Yes, but how? Terrific ideas! Excellent thinking! Superb insights! Great goals! 'Yes, but how?' How do I go about it?"[3] How do we more fully enter into the story of God's renewal of the earth? How do we embrace Advent hope?

There is no one right way to keep Advent. We need discernment to embrace God's invitation to us in each particular season of life. Yet, this is not to say that the ways we observe Advent should be entirely a matter of individual choice or preference. The church offers us practices and traditions that distinguish this season from Christmastide and help us answer "Yes, but how?" These practices give us ways to unwrap the gifts offered by the global and ancient church through Advent.

PRAYER, FASTING, AND ALMS

The best-known ways of marking Advent today are Advent wreaths and Advent calendars. These can be great resources, and our family enjoys them each year. But they are not the most pivotal disciplines of Advent. They also aren't the most traditional ones. They are recent additions from the last couple of centuries. So I'll begin with those key practices that have marked the season from its very beginning: prayer, fasting, and giving.

As long as Advent has existed, Christians have taken up this trio of habits to prepare their hearts for the three comings of Christ.

They are also addressed by Jesus himself in the Sermon on the Mount. In this sermon Jesus criticizes the way certain religious people engage in these disciplines (see Matthew 6:1-18). His words serve as a caution to us today. All these practices can become warped by being on public display. They can be used for our own ends—to seek approval from others or to become smugly self-satisfied. Jesus' warnings to not be conspicuously pious seem particularly relevant in the internet age, with the temptation to tweet or post about every experience, thought, donation, and devotional act. Social media, whatever else it is, is a medium that makes nearly everything performative, and Jesus tells us in the Sermon on the Mount that we must actively resist confusing devotion with performance.

But Jesus isn't telling his disciples not to pray, fast, or give. In fact, he seems to take it for granted that his followers *will* do these things regularly, since he gives his disciples instructions on what to do "when" (not "if") they do them. Instead, he recenters these acts on God.

For the early church these three spiritual disciplines—prayer, fasting, and giving—were held together. All three of them were robustly physical. Early church leaders spoke about them in almost medicinal terms: a way of healing our souls through how we use our bodies. To work on the body was also to work on the soul; to discipline the body was to purify the soul. Prayer, fasting, and giving are tangible ways to learn to follow Christ not only with our minds but with the entirety of our beings.

It's obvious how fasting and giving are embodied practices, but we don't always think of prayer in this same way. Yet when we look at how the early church thought about prayer, the sheer physicality of it is striking.

To begin with, prayer was almost always vocalized. Western Christians today rarely pray aloud unless we are praying with other people. In the early church, whether praying individually or corporately, prayer was spoken out loud. Christians also sought to pray facing east because Eden was understood as a garden planted in the east and early Christians saw the resurrection of Jesus as a returning to and restoration of Eden. Gregory of Nyssa in the fourth century said Christians should pray facing east because in prayer we are looking for and remembering paradise, our "ancient fatherland," our true home. Others like John of Damascus in the eighth century said we face east in anticipation of the dawning of the "sun of righteousness" (Malachi 4:2).[4]

Throughout church history, the posture in which one prayed was a pivotal part of prayer itself. Some early Christians stood when they prayed with hands raised (as Paul commends in 1 Timothy 2:8), or they knelt in imitation of Daniel (Daniel 6:10), or they lay prostrate like Moses (Deuteronomy 9:18-20). Early church prayer meetings looked more like a Pilates class than our staid, contemporary "moments of silence."

The time of day at which one prayed also mattered to the ancient church, and early Christians communally set apart specific hours of prayer (see Acts 3:1), a pattern known as fixed-hour prayer. This continues today in monasteries around the world. Fixed-hour prayer is also what gave birth to the Anglican prayer offices, with four set times of daily prayer.[5] The liturgical seasons played a role in shaping prayer as well. The penitential character of Advent and Lent, for instance, gave rise to a focus on confessional prayers during those months.[6]

We need not renovate modern prayer practices to be identical to those of the early church. God delights in prayer itself, not only if prayer resembles that of the ancients. Yet the prayers of those before us offer an invitation to grow in prayer.[7]

For a long time—well into adulthood—I thought prayer meant one thing: talking to God with words I came up with. That was all there was to it. So when I heard calls to "grow in prayer" I thought people were telling me to spend more and more *time* talking to God, which came to seem like an impossible burden. There are only so many hours in the day. At some point I need to sleep. I need to get dinner on the table. I need to get some work done and concentrate on other things. Plus, it doesn't take long for me to run out of things to say to God. It seemed I just wasn't wordy enough to grow in prayer (and I'm more than a little wordy).

As I've learned about different forms of prayer that have been handed down by the church, the call to grow in prayer became an invitation, not to shove more "quiet time" into a day but to explore different *ways* of praying. Each practice of prayer allows us a new glimpse into who God is and how to know and follow him.

Most Americans intuitively understand spiritual practices—including prayer and fasting—mostly in individualized and spiritualized ways. The point seems to be achieving a sense of personal peace or spiritual growth. These disciplines can certainly give us an experience of peace and aid growth, but for the early church they also had dramatic material and social consequences. Christian practices were taken up collectively and had a communal purpose and end.

Origen regarded prayer for the emperor as more effective to bring about justice than bloodshed on the battlefield. He counted those who pray as more essential to a nation than an army.[8] Similarly, fasting was not simply a means to grow in personal intimacy with God. It was an active commitment to join God

> to loose the chains of injustice
>> and untie the cords of the yoke,
> to set the oppressed free
>> and break every yoke . . .
> to share your food with the hungry
>> and to provide the poor wanderer with shelter.
>> (Isaiah 58:6-7)

Almsgiving was not simply a matter of charity but of justice—a recognition that God has provided wealth so that we would voluntarily redistribute it so that "there need be no poor people among you" (Deuteronomy 15:4). These practices, then, are earthy, practical, and embodied methods by which God moves us from focusing on our small, cramped, insular worlds to taking up God's priorities—joining him in bringing his kingdom to our neighborhoods and cities.

Fasting and almsgiving are closely connected in the Christian tradition—so much so that it's hard to pry them apart. Fasting is a way to experience solidarity with those who are hungry, but it's incomplete without also seeking to relieve their hunger. "What can be more efficacious than fasting? By its observance we draw near to God," preached Saint Leo the Great in the fifth century, "fasting has always been food for virtue." He continues, "But since our souls do not attain to salvation by fasting alone, let us supplement our fasting with acts of mercy toward the poor. Let us spend on virtue what we withhold from pleasure. Let abstinence on the part of someone fasting become nourishment for the poor. Let us put our efforts to the defense of widows, the advantage of orphans, the consolation of mourners, the reconciliation of rivals. Take in the stranger, relieve the oppressed, clothe the naked, care for the sick."[9]

This profound connection in the early church is an example for us today. Fasting calls us to a renewed commitment to loving our neighbors in practical ways. The money or time we save through fasting or abstaining from meals or some other activity (like screen time) we then use to serve others.

The reason the church recommends fasting during Advent isn't that Christians think the stuff of earth is bad or dirty. In Christmastime we are called to feast—and we should make sure our feasting, fun, and revelry surpass the intensity of our fasting and self-denial (and last all twelve days). Jesus fasted for prolonged periods, but he also enjoyed eating and drinking so much that he was criticized for it (see Matthew 11:19). The body, with its appetites for food, drink, sex, and sleep, is not bad. It is glorious. Every pleasure-sensing neuron in our bodies is a gift and testament that we were created for beauty, for joy, for eternal embodied feasting.

But bodily comforts and pleasures, as good as they are, can enslave us. Fasting is a way to take away the props, devices, and numbing agents that keep us from finding true comfort in God. By fasting we confess that food is good, but it is not the ultimate good.

Fasting is also a bodily exercise in humility. We lean into our own limitations and neediness. The historian of desert monasticism Gabriel Bunge wrote that fasting is not a good in its own right, but it "causes the soul to experience in a fundamental way its complete dependence upon God."[10]

So let's get really practical. Brass tacks. How should we fast during Advent?

First, Sundays are always feast days, even during penitential seasons like Advent and Lent. Every Sunday Christians celebrate the resurrection. So knock yourself out. If you've been abstaining from something during the week, indulge on Sundays.

Second, fasting can be complicated by our Western culture's disordered relationship with food. Some overindulge, while others are obsessed with dieting and sculpting the perfect body. There was a time not long ago when fasting was regarded as a strange act reserved for religious fanatics. Now intermittent fasting, juice cleanses, and health fasts are all the rage. It is hard to tease out when we are fasting in a way that builds reliance on God and solidarity with the suffering and when we're spiritualizing our attempt to get a beach bod by spring break or achieve such extreme levels of health that all other goods in our life are eclipsed. Of course, it makes sense that things that benefit us spiritually would also be good for our physical health. Nonetheless, we need to be intentionally discerning about our internal state so that we fast to experience hunger for God and not to feed our vanity, addictions, or obsessions.

This brings us to an important caveat. For those who have struggled with eating disorders, fasting can be a challenging subject. If you have or have had a disordered relationship with food, it may be in your best interest not to try fasting from food. Even in churches that require fasting (like in Eastern Orthodoxy) priests often ask those with a history of anorexia or bulimia to not abstain from food. There's freedom to skip fasting without any guilt.

How each of us takes up fasting falls squarely within the realm of wisdom, not ironclad law. There's no single prescription for fasting that's going to fit everyone.

There are also those (like me) who have certain health conditions that make fasting impossible, or at least trickier. I have chronic migraines, so the discipline of fasting has to look different for me. The first time I tried a true fast I ended up in the emergency room. I learned the hard way that this spiritual discipline needed to be tailored to my own unique bodily needs.

Typically, in the Christian tradition "fasting" and "abstinence" have different meanings.[11] Abstinence is refraining from a particular food or drink (such as not eating meat on Fridays) or a particular habit or activity (like giving up social media or television). Fasting is avoiding food altogether or eating a very limited diet—for example, a small bowl of rice and beans for the evening meal and a roll and a banana interspersed through the day; just enough food so you don't pass out or feel terrible, but few enough calories that you never feel full.

Still, I use these terms fairly interchangeably. If you need to eat normally during Advent and instead fast from Twitter, that is also a valuable spiritual practice. (And, of course, you can always fast from food and other things as well.)

Third, start small. Don't jump in headfirst. It will take a while for your body to adjust to fasting and for you to learn how your body responds to fasting. Fast for only one morning or one day. There's no Olympic medal for this. It's not meant to be a competition, much less an extreme sport. Begin gently.

Fourth, if possible, don't go it alone. Historically, fasting is most often practiced as a community. At certain times or seasons, churches fast or abstain from certain foods together. This helps people encourage one another as they fast. Our Eastern Orthodox friends abstain together from meat, dairy, and eggs before Easter and Christmas, so they also share vegan recipes and check in on each other throughout their time of fasting.

Last, hold fasting, prayer, and giving together. As we fast, we intentionally devote more attention to prayer. As you pray during Advent, it may help to experiment with new ways of prayer. Like the earliest Christians, you might pay attention to the physicality of prayer. Perhaps consider taking up fixed-hour prayer by praying one prayer office daily—maybe morning or evening prayer or compline.

If you are physically able, you might try kneeling, bowing, or lying prostrate as you pray. You might face east, like the early church, or make the sign of the cross before or after you pray. None of these are necessary in and of themselves, but they are part of the rich inheritance of Christian spirituality. They can enrich our prayers as we prepare ourselves for the coming of Christ.

We also seek ways to pursue justice and serve those who are in need as part of our discipline of fasting. One church I attended asked members to speak about one nonprofit organization or missions group that served "the least of these" each Sunday in Advent. It was a way we could recall works of justice and mercy happening around the world. Then the church took up a separate Advent offering to support the work of each organization. Advent should be a time when we stretch to be more generous than is comfortable. It's a time to give beyond our typical tithe to those who are most in need.

Recollection, Repentance, and Renewal

Advent falls toward the end of the Western year, but it marks the beginning of the church year. This timing provides the perfect vantage to reflect on the year behind and cultivate a renewed vision for the year ahead.

Many of us feel frenzied and busy. And many of us find ourselves uncomfortable with silence, stillness, and rest. Advent asks us to slow down and reflect.

Richard Foster once wrote that in our society the enemy majors in three things: "noise, hurry, and crowds." Thus, Foster goes on, "if we hope to move beyond the superficialities of our culture, including our religious culture, we must be willing to go down into the recreating silences, into the inner world of contemplation."[12] To practice Advent is to intentionally step away from noise, hurry, and crowds.

Advent exists so that every heart can "prepare him room." And this preparation cannot be merely an abstract idea. We prepare Christ room by rearranging our schedules to prioritize solitude, silence, contemplation, and reflection.

This doesn't mean we have to escape to the monastery (though if we can spend a few days in retreat, Advent is a great time to do so). Most of us have jobs or kids or other responsibilities that make stillness a challenge. But the call of Advent is to make space and time to be healed and renewed, even if it's only a few minutes a day.

One particularly helpful discipline during Advent is to take up praying the examen prayer. This form of prayer, which comes from the Ignatian tradition of Catholic spirituality, invites us to review and reflect on our day. During Advent I typically use the examen prayer to look back on the year behind. In the examen we take time to notice the gifts God has given us through the day (or year), times of joy and delight. We then express gratitude and reflect on what these moments reveal about ourselves and about

God. We also pay attention to where we felt desolate, alone, or abandoned by God, and where we fell into sin and self-reliance. We then confess and repent of our sins—a particularly vital practice in Advent—and invite God into these places of emptiness and pain in our lives.

But we don't have to overcomplicate it. Silence is as cheap and readily available as simply sitting in God's constant presence. Nothing more. Just sitting there. The hardest and easiest thing you'll do all day.

ADVENT CALENDARS AND WREATHS

Once the sole property of liturgical churchgoers, Advent has recently become trendy. The season owes its spike in popularity in large part to the rise of Advent calendars. Proving that there is nothing that cannot be commercialized, this traditionally penitential season now brings us untold branding options, including the Lego Harry Potter Advent Calendar ($32.82), the Barbie Advent Calendar ($29.99), and, for an elite set of grownups, the Tiffany & Co. Advent Calendar ($112,000).

The first Advent calendars were created by German Lutherans in the early twentieth century to count down the days from the beginning of Advent to Christmas. In 1908, in Munich, the printer Gerhard Lang created a design with colored pictures that became the prototype for today's Advent calendars. In the 1930s, the St. Johannis Printing company made Advent calendars with Bible verses, telling the Christmas story. It wasn't until after World War II, however, that Advent calendars became widely available around the world. Richard Sellmer Verlag of Stuttgart created the first mass-produced calendar in 1946, called "The Little Town," which was the original Advent calendar widely available in the United States.[13]

My family's yearly countdown through our Advent calendar—which we fill with chocolate treats (we know, we know, not so penitential)—has been a fun part of our Advent practice. Though it's admittedly in tension with the priority of fasting, this is our children's favorite part of the season. It's a tangible way to (quite literally) taste the anticipation that Advent highlights. We also pair the opening of the Advent calendar with short readings from Scripture and an Advent devotional for children each day. If it takes some sweets to entice our kids into the story of Scripture, so be it.

For as long as we have been Anglicans, my family has also made an Advent wreath each year, and I've grown to look forward to it gracing our kitchen table. Advent wreaths are most often a circle of four candles for each week of Advent leading to Christmas Eve. In the center is a white candle, the "Christ candle," which is lit during Christmastime. Each night we light the Advent candles together as a family, first one, then two, and so on till all four colored candles are lit on the fourth week of Advent.

No one is quite sure where the Advent wreath tradition comes from. The first time we see something that looks like it is in the nineteenth century (an extremely recent addition in the vast history of the church). A Lutheran pastor named Johann Hinrich Wichern, who started a home for orphans in 1833, created a wreath to help these children look forward to Christmas. Wichern's wreath was a wooden cartwheel covered in evergreen branches with four white candles for each Sunday of Advent and red candles for the other weekdays of Advent. The idea caught on among German churches, who put wreaths with four or five candles (one for each Sunday and then a Christ candle lit on Christmas) in the sanctuary during Advent. By the 1920s the practice had spread all over Germany. The tradition spread to the United States in the 1930s, and colored candles were added shortly thereafter.[14]

While the traditional and most common liturgical color used in Advent is purple, some churches use blue. There are several reasons for this, some historical and some aesthetic and practical.[15] An important theological reason blue is used is that it is the traditional color associated with Mary, so it colorfully recalls her waiting for the birth of her son during Advent. Some churches also like to use blue to distinguish Advent from Lent.

Yet most often three of the candles in the wreath are purple. Strikingly, on the third Sunday of Advent, for that one week only, the color changes. We light a pink candle. The minor key of Advent shifts slightly; the tone is subtly brighter. Things quite literally become rosier as purples are replaced with pinks—the liturgical color representing joy.

This third Sunday of Advent is called Gaudete Sunday. The name *Gaudete* is taken from the first word of the introit that begins eucharistic worship: *Gaudete in Domino semper*, "Rejoice in the Lord always." Typically, each Scripture reading on this Sunday is a call to joy, a reminder that things may look really dark in these short, late days of Advent, but hope is not lost. We have not been left alone in this sad world. Our king is indeed coming; a baby is on the way.

This experience of Gaudete Sunday—of lighting a candle of joy in the midst of the longest, darkest nights of the year—is the posture of all of our Christian life. Gaudete Sunday gives us a fresh breath of air. Its pink candle is a chromatic reminder that our groaning will soon end with birth; the fulfillment of all our collective waiting is soon to arrive.

Conclusion

Karl Barth wrote, "What other time or season can or will the Church ever have but that of Advent?"[1] Our Christian life is a long practice in waiting—waiting for God to meet us, to grow us, to save us. And, ultimately, waiting for Jesus to set all things right.

Our broader culture often conditions us to avoid the pain and uncertainty of waiting. If patience is a learned habit, so is impatience. If we are healthy, financially secure, and privileged, we can seek to meticulously rid our lives of waiting. With digital technology, we find information, buy things, share our thoughts and feelings, and plan our days in record time. We move at breakneck speed. We value—if not worship—efficiency, productivity, punctuality, and convenience. We dwell in an impatient culture. We collectively avoid the hard lessons found in waiting.

Yet there are some things we cannot speed up. There are limitations we cannot transcend. Children will always be tutors in inefficiency. My kids dawdle. They walk slowly. They are usually not concerned with my timeline and to-do list. If you want an exercise in patience, let a two-year-old put on their own shoes.

The aged also show us our addiction to hurry. My aging mother's pace has slowed. I must learn to take my time in order to walk with her. In many ways her pace of life is far more humane than mine.

Pregnancy is another apt metaphor for Advent. The growth of a child in the womb always involves waiting. When a woman is pregnant, she dwells in a daily mystery. She embodies both anticipation and surrender. Her body is an active part of gestation, of course. Yet ask any woman who's been pregnant and she'll tell you that, in many ways, she was just along for the ride. There is something larger than us that we simply participate in—something that calls all the shots. There's wonder beyond what we can name, measure, predict, or control.

One of my favorite Advent memories is when, over a decade ago, I was ordained on Saint Nicholas Day. I was eight-and-a-half months pregnant. With my shockingly swollen belly, my procession down the aisle of our church during the ordination service was more of a waddle than anything dignified or ceremonial. When the others I was ordained with lay prostrate before the cross (and the bishop), I could only kneel, with a kicking, hiccupping, somersaulting human being inside of me.

But what an apt picture of Advent.

My ordination process had been over five years long, with twists and turns, doubts and uncertainty, and lots of waiting along the way. Here was another step in that winding vocational path. Carrying this beloved child was a process of waiting, not knowing what would come. And we as a church were waiting together for the one to whom we prayed, the one who came as an infant, whose work continues in the world even now. We were waiting with the whole church, the world over and throughout time, through twists and turns, in yearning and hope, with so much history behind us and so much uncertainty ahead.

We can be tempted to focus exclusively on outcomes, to think what matters most is the end product, the resolve, the conclusion. We want to skip ahead. Waiting can seem like wasted time. But in that service, as the congregation sang *Veni Sancte Spiritus*, "Holy Spirit Come," what was clear is that the process matters. In the long process of ordination, I was being formed; a vocation was slowly being shaped and birthed. In all that time of waiting for labor, a child was being formed, quietly growing within me. And in our times of waiting, as individuals and as a church, what might God be growing?

Advent is training in hope because this season tells us that when things lie fallow they do not lie in waste; things that seem dormant are not dead, and times of waiting are not without meaning, purpose, or design. God is working, sometimes almost imperceptibly, deep beneath the surface of time. Waiting is part of his redemption. It is part of his gift to us. It is part of his grace.

"Above all, trust in the slow work of God," writes Teilhard De Chardin. "We are quite naturally impatient in everything to reach the end without delay. We should like to skip the intermediate stages. We are impatient of being on the way to something unknown, something new." But, he says, "Give Our Lord the benefit of believing that his hand is leading you, and accept the anxiety of feeling yourself in suspense and incomplete."[2]

Advent holds together many tensions—time and eternity, presence and absence, longing and fulfillment. It is, as John Calvin once said of the Eucharist, more to be experienced than to be understood.[3] Advent is not merely a collection of themes, Scriptures, practices, and prayers but a daily immersion in mystery, a lesson in grace learned through how we rub against time.

It asks us to accept the ache of being in suspense and incomplete. Yet Advent—and the waiting it represents— is not an end in itself. The whole point of this season is to prepare for the feasts ahead—the celebration of Christmas, the joy of God surprising us in the present, and the hushed awe when every knee finally bows before the coming king.

Someday all of our Advents will end. The wait will be over. The Lord will come. Yet all of our waiting—our struggles and sorrows, our doubts and fears, our days and weeks—will be a vital part of the story. It will be part of the "hallelujah" that echoes from a creation that once groaned. It will be part of the restoration of all things. It will be part of what is being born.

Until then we live each minute of our lives between Jesus' first advent in the nativity and his final advent. Until then we dwell in liminality, in the meantime.

As we both enjoy and endure this meantime, with all its beauty and suffering, with its bright sadness, Advent, like so many other spiritual practices, is merely a tool. It is meant to teach us how to live in hope and to trust and love the object of our hope. It is merely a tool, but it is one that has proven useful across many generations and many lives. May it prove useful in ours as well.

Blessed Advent to you.

And remember: our king is coming. Get ready.

Acknowledgments

I am grateful for the community that helped this book come to be.

Thank you to Esau McCaulley, who raised the idea of this series to me over the phone several years ago and invited me in. Esau and his family have become one of the most treasured gifts of our lives. He is the editor of this series but also my chief confidant in my writing life, and our many hours of conversation have helped me not only think and write better but hold to our shared hope all the more.

I am grateful for the work, culture, and people at InterVarsity Press, and it has been a privilege to partner with them on four books now. Special thanks to Ethan McCarthy, my patient and wise editor on this book.

Thank you to Steven Purcell and all the leadership and staff of Laity Lodge for providing nourishing and needed space to work on this manuscript. What a gift!

Thank you to the staff and congregants of Church of the Ascension in Pittsburgh and to Resurrection Anglican and Church of the Cross in Austin, Texas.

I am ever so grateful to Andy Crouch, who first floated the idea of writing this book with help from my husband, Jonathan, and whose advice and guidance throughout this project have been invaluable. Along with Andy, Andrea Dilley, Nii Addy, Michael Wear, and John Inazu walked with me (and listened to me complain, struggle, and figure out how to live and write) for the past few years with unending support, encouragement, and guidance. I could not make it without these friends and colaborers.

Thank you to Carley Reigle, who, as my husband says, keeps our life from falling into a dark abyss. Her steadfast faith, remarkable administrative talent, reliable cheerfulness, and keen insight have been invaluable to my life and work.

Thank you also to Woody Giles, to whom we dedicated this book.

I wrote this book with the help of my husband, Jonathan, who is breathtakingly brilliant but, more important, is a seeker of wisdom and giver of grace. Thank you, Jonathan, for your pivotal contributions to this book and for sticking with me.

The *New York Times*, *Christianity Today*, and *The Well* have all allowed me to write about, publish on, and explore Advent over many years. These pieces have shaped my thinking and this book.

I appreciate my editors at the *Times*, particularly Eleanor Barkhorn, Brian Zittel, and Peter Catipano for supporting me as a writer more generally and also for giving me time to finish this manuscript.

Jonathan and I together want to honor the memory of our former priest, Rev. Thomas McKenzie, who died tragically, along with his oldest child, as we were writing this book. I've quoted Thomas in all three of my books for adults, which speaks to how deeply his teaching has shaped our spiritual lives, impacted our relationship with God, and helped steer our vocations.

Jonathan and I also want to thank our three children, our most important collaborative projects. Raine, Flannery, and Gus, you have been patient and sacrificial as we've written and worked. Your smiles, questions, closeness, cuddles, energy, and lives are a source of overwhelming joy. You are also our very favorite people to practice Advent (and Christmas!) with. May you know Jesus as king, be ever on the ready for his return, and always hold to hope.

And glory be to the Word, the source of all our hope, from whom any goodness in our little words flows, and by whom they will be redeemed.

Notes

1. Yearning

[1] Fleming Rutledge, *Advent: The Once and Future Coming of Jesus Christ* (Grand Rapids, MI: Eerdmans, 2018), 5.

[2] Anglican Church in North America, The Book of Common Prayer (Huntington Beach, CA: Anglican Liturgy Press, 2019), 132. All references to the Book of Common Prayer are to the 2019 revision used by the Anglican Church in North America.

[3] Malcolm Guite, *Waiting on the Word: A Poem a Day for Advent, Christmas and Epiphany* (Norwich, UK: Canterbury Press, 2015), 67.

[4] This analogy of the liturgical calendar being like immersive theater is a common one. I first heard it from the late Rev. Thomas McKenzie and later heard Julie Canlis lecture on the idea at Hutchmoot in 2017. Alissa Wilkinson developed it in her essay "Advent, Explained," *Vox*, November 25, 2019, www.vox.com/culture/21805198/advent -explained-wreath-calendar-season-nazi-christmas-catholic. Tara Isabella Burton also has a lengthy exploration of immersive theater in *Strange Rites: New Religions for a Godless World* (New York: Public Affairs, 2020).

[5] Guite, *Waiting on the Word*, 67.

[6] See Tish Harrison Warren, "Having a Hard Christmas? Jesus Did Too," *New York Times*, December 25, 2022, www.nytimes.com/2022/12 /25/opinion/hard-christmas-jesus.html.

[7] Michael Horton, *People and Place: A Covenant Ecclesiology* (Louisville, KY: Westminster John Knox, 2008), 29.

[8] Rich Mullins, "Calling Out Your Name," *Songs*, Reunion, 1996.

[9] Book of Common Prayer, 133.

[10] N. T. Wright, "Reading Paul, Thinking Scripture," in *Scripture's Doctrine and Theology's Bible*, eds. Alan Torrance and Markus Bockmuehl (Grand Rapids, MI: Baker, 2008), 62.

[11] Rutledge, *Advent*, 5.

[12] Although "historic premillennialism" is a doctrine taught by many of the early church fathers, the idea of the "rapture" in premillennial dispensationalism is a nineteenth-century invention. See Charles Hill, *Regnum Caelorum: Patterns of Millennial Thought in Early Christianity* (Grand Rapids, MI: Eerdmans, 2001), for historic premillennialism, and for premillennial dispensationalism, see George Marsden, *Fundamentalism and American Culture* (New York: Oxford University Press, 1982), 51-55.

[13] Steve Garber, *Visions of Vocation: Common Grace for the Common Good* (Downers Grove, IL: InterVarsity Press, 2014), 203.

[14] Charles Riepe, quoted in *Advent: A Sourcebook*, ed. Thomas J. O'Gorman (Chicago: Liturgy Training Publications, 1988), 12.

2. Longing

[1] Adam English, *Christmas: Theological Anticipations* (Eugene, OR: Cascade, 2016), 71-73.

[2] Herbert Thurston, "Lent," Catholic Encyclopedia, New Advent, 1910, www.newadvent.org/cathen/09152a.htm.

[3] James MacKinnon, *The Advent Project* (Berkeley: University of California Press, 2000), 35.

[4] MacKinnon, *Advent Project*, 150-52.

[5] Bobby Gross, *Living the Christian Year* (Downers Grove, IL: InterVarsity Press, 2012), 37.

[6] Quoted in N. T. Wright, "Communion and Koinonia," *Pauline Perspectives: Essays on Paul 1978-2013* (Minneapolis, MN: Fortress, 2013), 269.

[7] St. Nikolai of Ochrid and Zica, *Prayers by the Lake*, trans. Rt. Rev. Archimandrite Todor Mika and Very Rev. Dr. Stevan Scott (Munster, IN: Ancient Faith Publishing, 2018), xxxiii, 57.

[8] For more on this theme, see Tish Harrison Warren, *Prayer in the Night* (Downers Grove, IL: InterVarsity Press, 2021).

[9] David Foster Wallace, *Infinite Jest* (New York: Little, Brown, 2009), 389.

[10] Maximus of Turin, *The Sermons of Maximus of Turin*, trans. Boniface Ramsey (New York: Newman Press, 1989), 144-45.

[11] John Breck, "Bright Sadness," Orthodox Church in America, May 1, 2005, www.oca.org/reflections/fr.-john-breck/bright-sadness.

[12] Remi Hoeckman, "The Ecological Degradation: A Challenge to Religious," *Angelicum* 67, no. 1 (1990): 68.

[13] John Climacus, *The Ladder of Divine Ascent*, trans. Colm Luibheld and Norman Russell (Mahwah, NJ: Paulist Press, 1982), 121.

[14] See, for instance, Genesis 8:17; 15:4-5; 35:11; Exodus 1:7; 1 Samuel 1; Isaiah 54, 56; Jeremiah 3:16; 23:3; Ezekiel 36:11; Luke 1:5-38.

[15] Baptism as a "womb" of new life is among the most common images used to understand the ritual in the early church. See Brian Spinks, *Early and Medieval Rituals and Theologies of Baptism* (New York: Routledge, 2006), and Tish Harrison Warren, "The Church Made Vagina Sculptures Long before Nadia Bolz-Weber," *Christianity Today*, February 26, 2019, www.christianitytoday.com/ct/2019/february-web-only/nadia-bolz-weber-church-made-vagina-sculptures.html.

3. CRYING OUT

[1] Robert Webber, *Ancient-Future Worship* (Grand Rapids, MI: Baker, 2008), 29-40.

[2] Alasdair MacIntyre, *After Virtue,* 2nd ed. (South Bend, IN: University of Notre Dame Press, 1984), 216.

[3] James K. A. Smith, *Imagining the Kingdom* (Grand Rapids, MI: Baker, 2013), 135.

[4] T. F. Torrance, "Salvation Is of the Jews," *Evangelical Quarterly* 22 (1950), 166.

[5] John F. A. Sawyer, *The Fifth Gospel: Isaiah in the History of Christianity* (Cambridge, UK: Cambridge University Press, 1996), 30.

[6] Ben Witherington III, *Isaiah Old and New: Exegesis, Intertextuality, and Hermeneutics* (Minneapolis: Fortress, 2017), 13.

[7] Quoted in Sawyer, *Fifth Gospel*, 1.

[8] The biblical scholar Tim Mackie of the Bible Project helpfully says, "The Bible is a unified story that leads to Jesus." "Our Mission," Bible Project, copyright 2022, https://bibleproject.com/about.

[9] Craig Bartholomew notes that the desert highway of Isaiah 35 is the highway that runs from Egypt to Assyria and that it already existed in Isaiah's day. "Indeed Israel had been perched precariously on it for centuries. But now it will function as highways should, not as a contested focus of power games but as a means for celebrating before Yahweh the wonderful diversity of his creation. Places and nations will not be obliterated, but will become what Yahweh always intended them to be." Craig Bartholomew, *Where Mortals Dwell* (Grand Rapids, MI: Baker, 2011), 85.

[10] Lauren Winner, *The Dangers of Christian Practice* (New Haven, CT: Yale University Press, 2018), 37.

[11] Richard Bauckham, *The Bible and Ecology* (Waco, TX: Baylor University Press, 2010), 123.

[12] John Wesley, "The Sermons of John Wesley—Sermon 60: The General Deliverance," Wesley Center Online, http://wesley.nnu.edu/john-wesley/the-sermons-of-john-wesley-1872-edition/sermon-60-the-general-deliverance, accessed December 24, 2022.

[13] Stephen Tompkins, *William Wilberforce: A Biography* (Grand Rapids, MI: Eerdmans, 2007), 207.

[14] Learn more about the important work of A Rocha at https://arocha.us. See also Tish Harrison Warren, "Why I'm Giving to This Environmental Group," *New York Times*, December 18, 2022. https://messaging-custom-newsletters.nytimes.com/template/oakv2?campaign_id=230&emc=edit_thw_20221218&instance_id=80452&nl=tish-harrison-warren&productCode=THW&regi_id=94358299&segment_id=120218&te=1&uri=nyt%3A%2F%2Fnewsletter%2F47835ece-d8a5-5400-9473-76584c9ffbc0&user_id=88baccb6cef9480c4dfb78c723d86c7c.

[15] Rutledge, *Advent*, 11.

[16] Rutledge, *Advent*, 243.

[17] For a visceral representation of this ghastly moment, see Lucas Cranach the Elder, "Plate with the Head of St. John the Baptist (Fragment)," Cranach Digital Archive, lucascranach.org/PRIVATE_NONE-P166, accessed December 21, 2022.

[18] Rutledge, *Advent*, 42.

[19] Aleksandr Solzhenitsyn, *The Gulag Archipelago*, vol. 2 (New York: Harper & Row, 1975), 615-16.

4. STIRRING

[1] I use the more popular translation, "The law of prayer is the law of belief," because it reads more succinctly. But Aidan Kavanaugh points out that the more accurate translation is, "The law of prayer establishes the law of belief"—the ordinary translation is not forceful enough.

[2] Aidan Kavanaugh, *On Liturgical Theology* (Collegeville, MN: Liturgical Press, 1984), 40.

[3] J. Neil Alexander, "The Shape of the Classical Prayer Book," in *The Oxford Guide to the Book of Common Prayer: A Worldwide Survey* (Oxford, UK: Oxford University Press, 2006), 71.

[4] See, for instance, John Fenwick and Bryan Spinks, *Worship in Transition: The Liturgical Movement in the 20th Century* (New York: Continuum, 1995).

[5] Leonel Mitchell, "Sanctifying Time: The Calendar," in *Oxford Guide to the Book of Common Prayer*, 479.

[6] Augustine, *Confessions*, trans. Henry Chadwick (Oxford, UK: Oxford University Press, 2008), 202.

[7] The Advent Collects can be found in Book of Common Prayer, 598-99.

[8] Oliver O'Donovan, *Self, World, and Time* (Grand Rapids, MI: Eerdmans, 2013), 9.

[9] O'Donovan, *Self, World, and Time*, 16.

[10] Cyril of Jerusalem, *The Catechetical Lectures of S. Cyril, Archbishop of Jerusalem*, 4th ed. (Eugene, OR: Wipf & Stock, 2021), 183-84.

[11] George Lawless, "*Desiderium Sinus Cordis Est*: Biblical Resonances in Augustine's '*Tractatus in Evangelium Iohannis* 40 §10," *Augustiniana* 48, no. 3/4 (1998): 305-29.

[12] James K. A. Smith, *How (Not) to Be Secular: Reading Charles Taylor* (Grand Rapids, MI: Eerdmans, 2014).

[13] Ben Witherington III, *Conflict and Community in Corinth: Socio-Rhetorical Commentary on 1 and 2 Corinthians* (Grand Rapids, MI: Eerdmans, 1995), 260.

[14] Paul Stanwood, "The Prayer Book as Literature," in *Oxford Guide to the Book of Common Prayer*, 145.

[15] Stanley Hauerwas, "Don't Lie," *No Small Endeavor* (blog), July 2017, www.nosmallendeavor.com/blog/hauerwas-do-not-lie.

[16] William Willimon, "Don't. Lie." *Peculiar Prophet* (blog), November 2, 2017, https://willwillimon.com/2017/11/02/dont-lie.

[17] Jaroslav Pelikan, *Mary Through the Centuries* (New Haven, CT: Yale University Press, 1998), 19-20, 157-61.

[18] Gerard Manley Hopkins, "The Blessed Virgin Compared to the Air We Breathe," Gerard Manley Hopkins website, updated February 20, 2019, https://hopkinspoetry.com/poem/the-blessed-virgin.

[19] See Esau McCaulley, "How the Coming of the Son Brings Hope to the Fatherless," *Christianity Today*, December 7, 2017, www.christianity today.com/ct/2017/december-web-only/how-coming-of-son -brings-hope-to-fatherless.html.

[20] Deirdre Joy Good, *Mariam, the Magdalen, and the Mother* (Bloomington: Indiana University Press, 2005), 64.

[21] Orthodox theology uses this term to describe how the light of Christ shines through the saints so that God is visible through them, an effect represented visually in iconography. The iconographer Solrunn Nes, for instance, writes that "the holy persons portrayed on an icon are illuminated from the inside and made translucent because their light comes from God himself" in Solrunn Nes, *The Mystical Language of Icons* (Grand Rapids, MI: Eerdmans, 2009), 24.

[22] This is Martin Luther's phrasing for the "unholy trinity" of the world, the flesh, and the devil. See Robert Jenson and Carl Braaten, eds., *Sin, Death, and the Devil* (Grand Rapids, MI: Eerdmans, 1999).

[23] This is Anthony Hoekema's preferred term for the traditional doctrine of "total depravity," which makes clear that the doctrine does not teach absolute corruption but corruption that permeates throughout all the human faculties. Anthony Hoekema, *Created in God's Image* (Grand Rapids, MI: Eerdmans, 1994), 150-52.

5. APPROACHING

[1] The nationwide "How soon can we listen to Christmas music?" debate can overshadow the reality that the church does have traditional Advent music. Of course, there is the big Advent hit "O Come, O Come, Emmanuel." But there is also "Come, Thou Long Expected Jesus," "Let All Mortal Flesh Keep Silence," "Savior of the Nations, Come," "Comfort, Comfort Ye My People," and many others. And Handel's *Messiah*, with its saturation in Old Testament prophecy and wide use of Scripture, is a beautiful way to mediate on the story of Advent. One year I spent time each Sunday of Advent listening to a

portion of *Messiah*. Whether or not we also listen to Christmas music during Advent, spending time with the music of Advent can help escort us into this season.

[2] Jared Patrick Boyd, *Invitations & Commitments: A Rule of Life* (self-published, 2014).

[3] Eugene Peterson, *Working the Angles: The Shape of Pastoral Integrity* (Grand Rapids, MI: Eerdmans, 1987), 16.

[4] This fascinating tradition is discussed in Gabriel Bunge, *Earthen Vessels: The Practice of Personal Prayer According to the Patristic Tradition* (San Francisco: Ignatius, 2010), 60-66.

[5] On the development of the hours of prayer see Robert Taft, *The Liturgy of the Hours in East and West* (Collegeville, MN: Liturgical Press, 1993).

[6] The Russian monk and spiritual director Ignatius Brianchaninov commends a discipline of prayer that includes a great deal of bowing and prostration, for instance. See Ignatius Brianchaninov, "The Arena: Guidelines for Spiritual and Monastic Life," in *Complete Works of St. Ignatius Brianchaninov*, trans. Nicholas Kotar (Jordanville, NY: Holy Trinity Publications, 2016).

[7] For more discussion, see Tish Harrison Warren, *Prayer in the Night* (Downers Grove, IL: InterVarsity Press, 2021).

[8] In his *Against Celsus* Origen writes, "We who by our prayers destroy all demons which stir up wars, violate oaths, and disturb the peace, are of more help to the emperors than those who seem to be doing the fighting." Origen, *Against Celsus* 8.73-75, in *Documents in Early Christian Thought*, ed. Mark Santer and Maurice Wiles (Cambridge, UK: Cambridge University Press, 1975), 229.

[9] Leo the Great, *Sermons*, trans. Jane Patricia Freeland and Agnes Josephine Conway, *The Fathers of the Church*, vol. 93 (Washington, DC: Catholic University of America Press, 1996), 54.

[10] Bunge, *Earthen Vessels*, 92.

[11] Order of the Holy Cross, *St. Augustine's Prayer Book* (Cincinnati, OH: Forward Movement, 2014), 3-4.

[12] Richard Foster, *The Celebration of Discipline* (New York: Harper Collins, 1988), 15.

[13] William D. Crump, *The Christmas Encyclopedia*, 3rd ed. (Jefferson, NC: McFarland & Co., 2013), 5.

[14] Crump, *Christmas Encyclopedia*, 6.

[15] Some Anglican churches use blue for Advent following the ancient practice of the diocese of Salisbury in England. The word for *Salisbury* in Latin is "Sarum," hence this liturgical color is sometimes called "Sarum blue." The scholar Vernon Staley notes that blue was also used in the English diocese of Bath and Wells. Vernon Staley, *The Liturgical Year* (London: Mowbray, 1907), 237.

CONCLUSION

[1] Karl Barth, *Church Dogmatics*, quoted in Fleming Rutledge, *Advent: The Once and Future Coming of Jesus Christ* (Grand Rapids, MI: Eerdmans, 2018), 57.

[2] Teilhard de Chardin, *The Making of a Mind: Letters from a Soldier-Priest, 1914-1919* (New York: Harper & Row, 1961), 57-58.

[3] John Calvin, *Institutes of the Christian Religion*, ed. John McNeill (Louisville: Westminster John Knox, 1960), 4.17.32.

The Fullness of Time Series

Each volume in the Fullness of Time series invites readers to engage with the riches of the church year, exploring the traditions, prayers, Scriptures, and rituals of the seasons of the church calendar.

LENT

Esau McCaulley

EASTER

Wesley Hill

PENTECOST

Emilio Alvarez

ADVENT

Tish Harrison Warren

CHRISTMAS

Emily Hunter McGowin

EPIPHANY

Fleming Rutledge